GOSPEL RADICALISM

GOSPEL
RADICALISM

The Hard Sayings
of Jesus

THADDÉE MATURA

Translated from the French by
Maggi Despot and Paul Lachance, O.F.M.

ORBIS BOOKS
Maryknoll, New York 10545

GILL AND MACMILLAN
Dublin

Originally published as *Le Radicalisme evangélique*, copyright © 1978 by Les Editions du Cerf, 29, bd Latour-Maubourg, Paris

English translation copyright © 1984 by Orbis Books, Maryknoll, N.Y. 10545
Published in the United States of America by Orbis Books, Maryknoll, N.Y. 10545
Published in Ireland by Gill and Macmillan Ltd, Goldenbridge, Dublin 8

Library of Congress Cataloging in Publication Data

Matura, Thaddée.
  Gospel radicalism.

  Translation of: Radicalisme évangélique.
  Bibliography: p.
  Includes index.
  1. Jesus Christ—Teachings.   2. Christian life—
Biblical teaching.   I. Title.
BS2417. C5M3413   1983   248.2'5   83–6249
ISBN 0–88344–182–9

Gill and Macmillan ISBN 7171-1334-5

+8.25
mat

Contents

PART THREE
OVERVIEW AND OPEN QUESTIONS

Introduction

The expression "gospel radicalism" receives mixed reactions. Some, insufficiently informed on the meaning of the words "radical" and "radicalism," do not see how secular and biblical terms could be related. Others believe that the political shading of the word "radicalism" carries more weight and that "radical" is the proper designation for what some call the "politics of Jesus."[1]

For those in biblical studies, and especially for religious who are questioning themselves on the meaning of their lives, the expression is a more familiar one. It is, in fact, the exegetes who first used those words to characterize certain aspects of the teachings of Jesus. In recent years the term has often occurred in writings on religious life. "Gospel radicalism" would define that life. Usually the texts on renunciation, poverty, the Beatitudes, and so forth are highlighted in order to illustrate and substantiate the expression. As far as I know, however, a cohesive presentation—analysis and synthesis—has never been done.

Called upon to reflect and write on religious life, I rapidly experienced the need to understand more precisely all that is entailed in this fashionable word, so often used but vaguely or never defined.[2] Thus while studying four years ago at the Ecumenical Institute of Tantur in Jerusalem, I undertook exegetical research on the theme of gospel radicalism. The following study is the result of that work.

One quickly notices that this study is essentially consecrated to the Synoptic Gospels, since they are the ones that transmit almost the totality of the "radical" sayings of Jesus. The other writings of the New Testament are studied only secondarily whenever parallel or similar texts can be found.

The method followed is a classical one. The historico-critical method, customary in this type of study, tries to grasp and explain

1

the original meaning and ultimate significance of the Gospel texts by situating them in their original setting, their communal evolution, and their redactional framework. The intent is a serious but not overly technical approach, which is obviously a balance not easily attained.

My approach and treatment of the subject of gospel radicalism are dictated by two factors: the special angle from which I envisage the theme, and the readers to whom it is directed. Once into the text, one sees that the angle chosen is a relatively narrow one. Indeed, to avoid being swamped by texts, I have from the beginning established a criterion of selection. The risk of such a choice is possibly a fragmented, disjointed point of view. I hope, though I cannot be certain, to have avoided that pitfall. I am aware of the extreme complexity of any biblical study. When one point is touched, all the others surface. Whoever dares to tug at the roots finishes by dragging along the whole tree. If, through our limited perspective, the reader perceives that there is more and that the horizon must be extended, all the better.

This study counts on attracting not only those "in the trade," exegetes, but also hopes to reach a larger public—all those who, for one reason or another, are aware of the theme of radicalism. Those people are, on the one hand, the religious, who are constantly being reminded that they are to live the gospel radicalism. (Perhaps they will be disappointed to discover that they have no monopoly here.) On the other hand, it is truly all Christians who must ask themselves whether the radical demands of Jesus are relevant and valid in their lives too.

I have such a public in mind—on the condition that they consent to the necessary attentive reflection. Thus I have sought, insofar as it was possible, to avoid technical erudition and voluminous notes. I have attempted to concentrate the study on the essential points, leaving aside what was not directly connected with the subject. Hence, because I hope to make this presentation pedagogically sound with frequent summaries and unavoidable repetitions, some will no doubt judge it too scholarly.

I know that I risk leaving everyone unsatisfied. The specialists will find the study too superficial and not sufficiently substantiated. Less initiated readers will find it arduous and arid. To everyone I would advise reading this book with the Gospels in hand, especially for Part Two. To become accustomed to the analysis and to approach the texts with an open mind, one could pass from Part One to Part Three and then return to the pièce de résistance, which is Part Two.

The particular angle proposed here is not found in any other study. (A selected bibliography gives more detailed indications on this point.) I mean to say that this is a pioneer work—inevitably with limitations—which includes a somewhat naive boldness and many false steps. One has the impression of unlocking the door to a new world. That sense of discovery is all the more heightened in that the subject is not a specific text or biblical theme. Rather, it is a question of applying to the gospel an expression or a "grid" that is derived from science or politics. Such is the origin of the word "radicalism." I simply hope to pave the way. Others, if only by opposition, will move beyond and do better.

Essential to me was first to see and then to show what honestly could be labeled "radical, radicalism" once applied to the gospel. I gradually discovered that, first, the entire gospel is, in a certain sense, radical. The demands said to be radical are the cutting edge of the message of Jesus. Second, those radical demands (far more extensive than merely the command to "sell one's goods and give them to the poor") are directed, at least in the Gospels, not to a special category of people, whoever they may be, but to the totality of believers. The radicalism embraces all of Christian existence and it challenges all those who commit themselves to it. That is the conclusion of this book, which strives to remain strictly exegetical.

NOTES

1. "It seems then that Fernando Belo questions himself on the human radicalism of the politics of Jesus of Nazareth, who would make of his liberating struggle a demonstration of unique power," writes A. Dumas in *Le Monde* (Nov. 2, 1977, p. 2), referring to the book by F. Belo, *Lecture matérialiste de l'évangile de Marc* (Paris: Cerf, 1974). Eng. trans.: *A Materialist Reading of the Gospel of Mark*, trans. Matthew J. O'Connell (Maryknoll, N.Y.: Orbis Books, 1981).

2. See Thaddée Matura, *Celibacy and Community,* trans. Paul Lachance and Paul Schwartz (Chicago: Franciscan Herald Press, 1973); "La vie religieuse dans un monde areligieux," *Nouvelle Revue Théologique* 99 (1977): 51–61.

PART ONE

CHOICE AND PRESENTATION
OF THE TEXTS

1

Vocabulary and Criteria for Our Choices

Words have an uneven life and history. Some seem to survive the test of time and remain faithful to their primal meaning, for example, the words "father," "mother," "bread," "wine." Others undergo a more stormy passage, unexpectedly appearing, quickly popularized, then slowly but inexorably fading. The current use of "witness" in the Christian sense of the word illustrates this point.

DIFFERENT MEANINGS OF THE WORD "RADICAL"

The word "radical," as both noun and adjective (the derivatives of which are "radicalism," "radicality," "radically," "radicalize"), is a relatively recent word, originating in the fifteenth century. Used initially in medieval medicine, in science (mathematics, geometry, astronomy, chemistry, botany), and in philology, it was eventually applied to politics and finally to exegesis and theology. We would stray far afield from our topic if we were to write a complete history of the evolution and metamorphosis of the word.

1. THE SECULAR MEANING[1]

Let us look, nonetheless, at the major phases of this evolution. The word "radical" (and its derivatives) is derived from the Latin word *radix* ("root") whose initial meaning pertains to the root of

7

a thing or a being. This is the basis for the word's scientific use as in mathematics, geometry, philology, and so forth, designating what is linked with the principle or essence of a thing. Subsequently the word has come to be used to express what is basic, fundamental and, by extension, absolute and complete.

In seventeenth-century England the term "radical" was applied to the field of politics. One talked about radical reforms—that is, total, fundamental reforms returning to the roots of a situation. English politicians of this leaning (left-wing liberals) were called radicals. In France the same name was given to the Republicans, partisans of "radical" reforms, organized in part after the fall of the Second Empire. Finally, in 1901 the Radical-Socialist party was organized in France and still exists today, with this name.[2] In the political context the expressions "radical," "radically," and "radicalism" thus acquired new life. These qualified the tendencies that were directed, at least theoretically, toward drastic reforms, tendencies that today we would call "revolutionary" as opposed to "liberal."

Since such developments "radical" has meant that which diverges from ordinary behavior or customs, that which is extreme, drastic, and hard. Radicalism purports to "approach all problems at their source, make a clean sweep of the established facts" (Robert) and "make extreme changes in existing views, habits, conditions, or institutions" (Webster).

2. THE RELIGIOUS MEANING

Lacking a complete study of the application of this term to the religious and, in particular, the exegetical field, we need to be satisfied with a few points of reference.

Rudolf Bultmann is the first, as far as I know, to make abundant use of the term. In his book *Jesus and the Word* (first published in German in 1926,[3] the great German exegete writes about the will of God which Jesus exposes through his preaching and to which he demands obedience. This obedience, which, Bultmann writes, "Jesus has conceived radically" (p. 73), forms the core of Jesus' ethic. This "radically conceived idea" (p. 77) is a "radical obedience," because "man inwardly assents to what is required of him . . . the whole man *in* what he does . . . is essentially obedient" (p. 77). Thus, for Bultmann, it is not this or that particular demand of Jesus that is radical. Rather, radical obedience is the way in which individuals incorporate the will of God into the roots of their being.

Thirty years after Bultmann's work, Herbert Braun, a disciple of Bultmann, published a study entitled *Radicalism in Late Dissident Judaism and in Primitive Christianity*.[4] Without giving a systematic definition of what he means by radicalism, he nevertheless provides a very detailed description of it. In a comparison of talmudic Judaism, the Qumran group, and the Essene texts with the teachings of Jesus, Braun shows through detailed analysis the attitude of each group toward the Law in general (radical obedience) and the particular demands made on them: rites, renunciation of goods, attitudes toward one's neighbor, martyrdom, and marriage. By using the term in the title of a book and making a comparative in-depth study of the components of what he considers "radicalism," Braun established the term in the world of exegesis.

In the French exegetical world the expression "radicalism," and in particular "gospel radicality," already used in the 1960s in the translation of a book by Rudolf Schnackenburg,[5] made a massive entry around the year 1970. In 1971 Beda Rigaux published an article entitled "The Radicalism of the Kingdom" in which, after indicating its basis in the following of Jesus, he analyzes Jesus' teachings and their "serious expression, where paradox and polemic forge the harsh formulas, thus marking the teaching and call of the gospel with gravity, seriousness, even tragedy."[6]

A typical and frequent use of the word can be found in a historical and theological article by J. M. R. Tillard, "Le fondement évangélique de la vie religieuse" (1969).[7] For Tillard it is the choice "for the crest of the wave of gospel radicality," or again, it is "gospel radicality institutionalized and become an inner law," which defines religious life. This is likewise the opinion of J. M. van Cangh in a 1973 text that treats the same question from an exegetical point of view.[8] Evidently such an application was immediately successful. A document by Pope Paul VI made use of it when he spoke of religious who "represent the Church insofar as she desires to commit herself to the radical demands of the Beatitudes."[9]

Thus if strictly exegetical studies reserve this term for a certain number of demands proposed by the Gospels, theological texts apply it mainly to the area of religious life. This quick overview of the word's religious use and meaning shows that the term "radicalism" usually designates the teachings of Jesus related by the Gospels, teachings that are especially rigorous and demanding, and hence radical.[10]

CRITERIA FOR OUR CHOICES

These linguistic data help us to find criteria better to define the object of our study. Not finding in the Gospels or elsewhere in the Bible the words "radical" or "radicalism" ("root," "to be rooted in," which are used in the Bible, have no relationship to their modern derivatives), other criteria are needed to search for, assemble, and analyze the texts.

The meaning drawn thus far from our inquiry into the word already orients our research. The texts to be studied will be those that propose or demand radical behavior—that is, attitudes or deeds diverging from ordinary (human or religious) ways of acting. The totality of these demands, related to a certain type of conduct, constitutes gospel radicality.

Certainly the choice of such criteria may seem arbitrary. Yet it is impossible to advance through the thicket of New Testament texts without a path to follow. In choosing as criteria the radical demands in the area of human behavior, I surely limit my approach, but perhaps the clarity and precision gained will prove well worth it.

My purpose, then, is to make an inventory, to classify, analyze, and interpret exegetically the ethical teachings of Jesus bearing radical traits—that is, unusual, paradoxical, decisive, or absolute characteristics. Once this step is completed, general conclusions can be drawn, bringing more light to bear on the content of gospel radicalism and on those for whom it is intended.

Such a choice, then, indicates the limitations of this study. It concentrates almost exclusively on the teachings of Jesus related in the Synoptic Gospels, since John's Gospel and the Pauline epistles contain few texts that, strictly speaking, can be considered radical. At the end of this study I shall say why this is so, what this means, and whether there are other radicalisms than the one presented in the Synoptics.

The intent of this research is not to cover everything that could qualify as radical in God, Jesus, or this or that situation (for example, the fact that the salvation of God is addressed first of all to the little ones, sinners, and the poor reveals a radicality of love in God and in Jesus). I wanted to limit my inquiry to the requirements of individual behavior and the radicalism of decision and deed to which one is called.

NOTES

1. P. Robert, *Dictionnaire alphabétique et analytique de la langue française* (Paris: Societé du Nouveau Littré, 1960), 5:752; *The Oxford Dictionary* (London: Oxford University Press, 1970), 8:99–100; *Webster's Third New International Dictionary of the English Language, Unabridged* (Chicago, 1966), 2:1872. These three dictionaries show no awareness of the religious meaning of the word.

2. ". . . radical current incarnating an intransigent or uncompromising fidelity to the memory of the French revolution. . . . Moreover, for a long time, only faint differences and a more pronounced intransigency distinguished the radicals from the rest of the Republican party" (J. Th. Nordman, *Le Monde*, June 23, 1976).

3. Rudolf Bultmann, *Jesus* (Tübingen: J. C. B. Mohr, 1926). English trans.: *Jesus and the Word* (New York: Charles Scribner's Sons, 1958). Quotations are taken from the English edition.

4. Herbert Braun, *Spätjüdisch—häretischer und früchristlicher Radikalismus*, 2 vols. (Tübingen: J. C. B. Mohr, 1969). First published in 1957.

5. Rudolf Schnackenburg, *The Moral Teaching of the New Testament* (New York: Herder and Herder, 1965); see "Jesus' Radicalism," pp. 73–81. The German original: *Die Sittliche Botschaft des Neuen Testamentes* (Munich: M. Hüber, 1954).

6. Beda Rigaux, "The Radicalism of the Kingdom," in *Gospel Poverty* (Chicago: Franciscan Herald Press, 1977), p. 122.

7. J.-M.-R. Tillard, "Le fondement évangélique de la vie religieuse," *Nouvelle Revue Théologique* 91 (1969): 933.

8. J. M. van Cangh, "Fondement évangélique de la vie religieuse,"

Nouvelle Revue Théologique 95 (1973): 635–47. "Religious life definitively makes a radical attitude, required of every Christian in particular situations, permanent and concentrated" (p. 644).

9. Paul VI, exhortation "Evangelii nuntiandi" of Dec. 8, 1975, in *The Pope Speaks* (1975), 21:39.

10. An example of the exegetical use of "radical": "One word to describe the teaching preserved in Q would be radical. It presents an absolute ethic conceived to register the immediate impact of the divine demand, uninfluenced by the contingencies of experience or the crippling realities of circumstances . . . the uncompromising character of their claim in its nakedness" (W. D. Davies, *The Sermon on the Mount* [Cambridge: Cambridge University Press, 1964], p. 107).

2

Presentation of the Radical Texts

So as not to confine ourselves to generalities, we now wish to present as completely as possible the texts that the criteria already presented permit us to consider as radical.* Various approaches are possible. One can follow the order of the Gospels, chapter by chapter, or group the texts according to collections of sayings or "constellations" to which these are connected, or finally, classify them in logical order.

To clarify and simplify matters, we shall not adopt the first approach because its result would be incoherent and fragmented. The second approach (the only one conforming to the literary structure of the Gospels and the message of the redactors) will be presented in depth later in our text.

The logical classification (the third approach just mentioned) offers the most appropriate beginning and first contact with the totality of the texts. Its advantage is our familiarity with it, accus-

*In the following pages, references to Mark without any further qualification always indicate passages common to the three Synoptics (the triple tradition); references to Matthew indicate passages he has in common with Luke (the double tradition, or Q); references to Luke indicate passages unique to him. The exceptions will be noted in passing unless the immediate context renders such an indication superfluous.

[Usually Matura translated the texts directly from the Greek. While following his emphases as closely as possible we chose nevertheless to use recognized translations of the Bible. Unless otherwise noted, all passages cited come from the Jerusalem Bible. —TRANS.]

tomed as we are to Greek logic (rational, orderly thinking). Moreover, it embraces a meditative, spiritual style in which texts of diverse origins are assembled in order to see them at a single glance. Such an approach is certainly arbitrary and occasionally does violence to a text. But it is used here only as a preliminary inventory of texts that will later be replaced in their original context for analysis.

LOGICAL CLASSIFICATION

Let us try to record most of the Gospel sayings making radical demands by grouping them according to a few logical centers of thought.

1. RADICAL PERSONALITIES

Before collecting the sayings expressing blunt and unusual demands, it is appropriate to note two Gospel personalities, John the Baptist and Jesus, whose behavior seems, at least at first glance, radical.

The Baptist

As soon as he appears in the Jordan desert, John the Baptist is presented clothed in prophetic garb (a camel-hair garment with a leather belt), living on locusts and wild honey (Mark 1:6). It is difficult to know whether his behavior suggests the personality of a prophet or that of an ascetic. Jesus' words contrasting John's clothes with the soft clothes of palace courtesans (Matt.11:8) and his words on John neither eating nor drinking (Matt. 11:8) tend to make us subscribe to the second hypothesis. Solitary, without family, clothed in coarse garb, practicing extreme eating habits, John would thus be an ascetic model unique in the New Testament.

Jesus

Although he actually praises John (Matt. 11:7–11), Jesus dissociates himself from this model. Jesus drinks, eats, and sits at the table of sinners (Mark 2:16), to the extent that he is even accused of being a glutton and a drunkard (Matt. 11:19). Also, on other points Jesus adopted attitudes clearly breaking from the usual behavior and habits of religious Jews.

Luke, who describes Jesus' birthplace as poor and away from his home (Luke 2:7), attributes to Jesus, beginning with his childhood, a high level of independence from his parents (Luke 2: 41–52). Mark (3:20–21) echoes this in the sharp opposition between Jesus and his family, which seems to prevent him from accomplishing his mission. Oddly omitted by Matthew and Luke, this episode explains well Jesus' declaration about his spiritual family being constituted only by those who do the will of God—a declaration reported by the Synoptics (Mark 3:31–35). Even if Luke (Acts 1:14) and John (John 2:1–5: Mary at the wedding feast in Cana; 19:25: Mary at the foot of the cross) make an exception for Mary, Jesus is presented as having broken from his family in Nazareth.

Jesus' sayings on the Son of man "having nowhere to lay his head" (Matt. 8:20) allude to the fact that the itinerancy and insecurity of his life is more than that of wild animals.

Jesus' inner attitudes toward God and people could also be read and interpreted through the "grid" of radicalism. Here we shall take only the most striking expressions of his desire to serve, become a martyr, and forgive his enemies. Jesus is not haughty or domineering as human rulers can be; he is "gentle and humble in heart" (only Matt. 11:29). Although he is the greater, the one who presides at table, he makes himself the servant (Luke 22:27). Mark 10:45 and Matthew 20:28 emphasize the same idea: Jesus has come not to be served but to serve, and to give his life as a ransom for many. His destiny is to give his life, drink the cup that he must drink (Mark 10:38 and Matt. 20:22), and be baptized with the baptism with which he must be baptized (Mark 10:38–39; Luke 12:50). He strains with all his being for this hour (Luke 12:50). Finally, on the cross, he puts into practice his own teaching concerning love of enemies (Matt. 5:43–48) by praying for his executioners and finding excuses for them (Luke 23:34).

Our concern being the study of the radical demands of Jesus, we have merely touched upon certain traits indicative of the Lord's personality. These traits, however, indicate the meaning and orientation of Jesus' teachings.

2. OVERALL RADICALITY OF JESUS' DEMANDS

No doubt Jesus calls to himself those who are overburdened and offers them rest (only Matt. 11:28–29), but he does not blunt the cutting edge of his demands. He has not come to bring peace but the sword and even division within families (Matt. 10:34–36). The road and the gate that lead to life are hard and narrow (Matt. 7:13–14). A great effort, even violence, is necessary to grasp the kingdom (Matt. 11:12). To enter it, the most painful sacrifices are called for: tear out your eye or cut off your right hand (Mark 9:43–47; Matt. 18:8–9). Before starting to follow Jesus, one must carefully weigh the cost that such a step demands (Luke 14:28–32). Once committed, one can no longer hesitate or look back (Luke 9:62). In short, an effort and an ongoing tension are required. Nothing is decided ahead of time, for if "many are called, few are chosen" (only Matt. 22:14).

3. DEMANDS OF THE SELF

What is demanded of disciples is truly unheard of. They must renounce themselves (Mark 8:34), hate themselves (Luke 14:25); rather than seeking to save their life, they must accept losing it (a saying quoted six times in the Gospels: Mark 8:35; Matt. 10:39; John 12:25). Called upon to suffer family opposition (Mark 13:12), hate, persecution, and even death for Jesus' sake (Mark 13:9, 12, 13), they must declare themselves for him in the presence of others (Matt. 10:32), even at the risk of their life (Matt. 10:28). For to take one's cross and follow Jesus (a saying repeated five times: Mark 8:34; Matt. 10:38), ultimately means that one must be ready even for a brutal death for his sake. It is difficult, even impossible, to ask for more from a person, since there is nothing more precious than one's being and life (Mark 8:36–37; Matt. 16:26). Even this, however, one must lose for the sake of Jesus.

Moreover, whatever good one does (almsgiving, fasting, prayer) is not done to be seen by others in order to receive their compliments. God, who sees all that is done in secret, will alone reward that one (only Matt. 6:1–6, 16–18). And when they have accomplished all they have been told to do by their master, they will have no right to any reward but will consider themselves "merely servants" (Luke 17:7–10).

4. ATTITUDES TOWARD ONE'S NEIGHBOR

Going beyond the demands of the Law, Jesus' disciples must not only not kill but must even avoid anger and abusive language (only Matt. 5:21–25). They must not judge (Matt. 7:1), condemn their neighbor (Luke 6:37), or resist the wicked (only Matt. 5:39). They must offer their left cheek to those who strike them on the right, give their cloak to those who want their tunic (Matt. 5: 39–40), and go two miles if someone orders them to go only one (only Matt. 5:41). They must give to anyone who asks and not turn away anyone who wishes to borrow (Matt. 5:42). As men and women of peace (Matt. 5:25), they must strive to be reconciled as soon as possible with their adversary (Matt. 5:42); they must always be ready to forgive (Mark 11:25; Matt. 6:14) and do so indefinitely (Matt. 18:21-22). Thus they will be merciful (only Matt. 5:7), for Jesus' commandments require that one loves the stranger and even the enemy (Matt. 5:43–47).

The disciple's word ought to be so straightforward and clear— a Yes or a No—that any oath or testimony is superfluous (Matt. 5:33–37).

Among Jesus' disciples, some (the twelve "apostles") were specially chosen and entrusted with a special mission (Mark 3: 13–19). Because of that privilege, they could be tempted to seek the first places, to succumb to the will to power (Mark 9:33–34; Mark 10:37; Matt. 20:21). Jesus suggests a conduct radically opposed to the powerful of the world and of religion. As he himself came to serve and not to be served (Mark 10:45), they are to be as servants, slaves, little ones (Mark 10:42-44), as defenseless and dependent as children (only Mark 10:14; Matt. 18:3-4). This is why there is no place in the community of disciples for honorary titles such as Father, Mother, Doctor (Matt. 23:8-10).

5. SPECIFIC RENUNCIATIONS

If after this very general listing, one moves to the specific moments of those radical choices, one notices that they crystallize around two poles of thought: family and material goods.

The Family

For those he calls to follow him, Jesus demands a break from family bonds; an on-the-spot decision to follow prevails over the serious and sacred duties to parents (Matt. 8:22). The disciples will often bear the brunt of family opposition and persecution (Matt. 10:34–36). Luke writes that the one who does not "hate" father, mother, wife, children, brothers, and sisters cannot be a disciple (Luke 14:26). As a matter of fact, the first ones called leave father and fellow workers to be with Jesus (Mark 1:20; Matt. 4:22). Those who have left all will receive eternal life and a new family (Mark 10:29–30). One of Jesus' sayings reported by only Matthew (19:10–12) and another particular saying in Luke 14:26; 18:29 (where "women" is added to the list of family members who must be renounced) suggest that one can totally renounce marriage for the sake of the kingdom of heaven.

Material Goods

Distrust of wealth, an obstacle for the believer to receive the Word, clearly emerges in Jesus' teachings (Mark 4:19: "lure of riches"). In effect it is difficult for the rich to enter the kingdom of heaven (Mark 10:23). Luke even relates a curse addressed to the rich (Luke 6:24). It is Luke, "the evangelist of the poor," who groups Jesus' teachings on this theme into well-ordered collections and who stresses their radicalism. Later on, we shall offer a detailed presentation of these Lucan texts; for now, let us simply indicate a few of the more incisive ones: one cannot be Jesus' disciple unless one renounces all of one's possessions (Luke 14:33), sells them, and gives them as alms (Luke 12:33).

As a matter of fact, Peter, Andrew, James, John (Mark 1:16–20), and Levi (Mark 2:13–14) leave behind their boats, nets, and tax-collecting table when Jesus calls them to follow him. Jesus explicitly asks prospective disciples to sell what they own and give it to the poor (Matt. 10:17–22) before they may join him. When sent on mission, the disciples must leave with neither gold, silver, coppers for their purses, haversack, bread, nor two tunics (Mark 6:8–9). Those who receive their message will provide for their needs (Matt. 10:10; Luke 10:7). All those who have thus left behind houses and land in this way are promised an abundant reward (Mark 10:29).

REGROUPING THE SYNOPTIC SAYINGS

The lists of texts and their logical classification have given us an idea of the force of Jesus' demands and their radicality. But this approach, useful as it is, has not taken into account the dynamics within the Gospels themselves. In order to tighten our analysis and see Jesus' sayings in their organic context, we must look at the collections in which they appear. Returning a second time in a different order to the texts that have just been presented will give the impression of *déjà vu*. It is nonetheless necessary.

Except for a certain number of independent sayings, scattered here and there, most of the texts listed are part of collections of sayings—at least so it seems. They are crystallized around a few poles of thought: (1) the theme of discipleship; (2) the collections on renunciation; (3) the collections on wealth and poverty; (4) the radicalization of the Law in the Sermon on the Mount.

1. DISCIPLESHIP

A certain number of radical sayings are, strictly speaking, bound up with the theme of discipleship. We know that Jesus called twelve men to follow him (Mark 3:13-19), twelve men who shared his life, received his teaching, and were entrusted with a mission and special authority. The very specific demands of renunciation are assembled around the narratives (or collections of narratives) relating to the vocation of the disciples, their mission, and their behavior as leaders.

Vocation Narratives

When Jesus calls some of the disciples (Mark 1:17-20; 2:13-17), we see them carry out actual acts of renunciation and leave their families and possessions. Apparently it is to eventual disciples that the exorbitant demands to follow the itinerant Jesus, who has no place to lay his head, to neglect the duty to bury one's own parents (Matt. 8:18-22), or to leave behind one's own people (Luke 9:60-62) are proposed.

Missionary Discourses

Mission, with its demands of poverty and insecurity, concern both the twelve (Mark 6:8-9) and the seventy-two disciples (Luke 10:9). They are the ones who will bear the brunt of family opposition (Mark 13:12), everyone's hate (Mark 13:13), persecutions, and even death (Mark 13:12). For Jesus has not come to bring peace but the sword and division—even in the family setting

(Matt. 10:34–36). These demands connected with poverty and persecution are precisely the ones Matthew inserts into what is called the "missionary discourse" (Matt. 10:1–12).

Humility and Service

Jesus' instructions that propose a child as a model of conduct are also directed to the disciples (Mark 10:13–16). Likewise, in the episode when the disciples argue among themselves as to who is the greatest (Mark 9:33–37), Jesus affirms that the greatest are the least, the last, the servants, or again that those who are first, the great ones, the leaders, must become servants and be like slaves, contrary to the ways of the powerful of the world (cf. the request of the sons of Zebedee: Mark 10:41–45). One sees these teachings on humility and service appearing in three different collections also directed to the disciples as a warning against the will to power.

The disciples, when in positions of authority and teaching roles, must refuse the titles of Rabbi, Doctor, Father, which one might want to give them (Matt. 23:8–12). And when they have accomplished everything asked of them, they will only deem themselves useless servants and unworthy of any reward (Luke 17:10).

2. RENUNCIATION

The sayings that have just been presented concern the entire group of disciples either directly or indirectly. Other collections are directed, with some distinctions, to all the hearers of Jesus' words.

The first, common to the three Synoptics (Mark 8:34–9:1), brings together the hardest sayings of Jesus on renouncing oneself, taking up one's cross, and losing one's life. Another collection, peculiar to Matthew and Luke, insists on the absolute priority of Jesus over the family and oneself, and insists on the necessity of taking up one's cross (Matt. 10:37–39). Luke adds the demand of renouncing all one's possessions (Luke 14:33) as well as the duty of carefully counting the cost before committing oneself (Luke 14:28–32).

Finally, it is fitting, in my opinion, to mention here the mysterious logion on the voluntary eunuchs (only Matt. 19:10–12), which must be understood as an invitation addressed freely to all to renounce marriage for the sake of the kingdom.

3. MATERIAL POSSESSIONS

The teachings on material possessions are grouped into three series: the first is common to all three Synoptics; the second, to Matthew and Luke; and the third belongs to Luke alone.

The Synoptic Collection

This group is well organized and identical in all three Gospels. Mentioned first is the rich man, who is called to sell everything he owns and to follow Jesus but who refuses because of his great wealth. After this are descriptions of how difficult it is for the rich to enter the kingdom of God (Mark 10:23–27) and the reward reserved for those who leave behind family and possessions (Mark 10:23–31).

Collections Common to Matthew and Luke

Let us first of all mention the slightly different forms of the Beatitude on poverty in these two Gospels (Matt. 5:3) and also the parallel notions of the good news proclaimed to the poor (Matt. 11:5).

In the Sermon on the Mount, Matthew presents a group of sayings followed by teachings on storing up real, true treasures (Matt. 6:19–21); the sound or healthy eye (Matt. 6:22–23); God and mammon (Matt. 6:24); and anxiety about material security (Matt. 6:25–34). All these pericopes are concerned with the attitude toward wealth. These texts are also found in Luke, but in three different contexts (cf. Luke 11:34–36; 12:22–34; 16:13).

Texts Peculiar to Luke

Luke offers abundant material on this theme. In addition to what is common to Matthew and Mark, Luke presents two collections that are peculiar to his Gospel and also several scattered logia.

The first collection is found in Luke 12:13–34. Part of this collection (vv. 22–34) has a parallel in Matthew, as we have just seen, but a dozen verses (13–21) are peculiar to Luke. This is the case, notably, for the warning against greed (12:13–15), illustrated by the parable of the foolish rich man and the poor man Lazarus (16:19–31). Likewise, verse 33 ("sell what you have and give alms") has no corresponding section in Matthew.

The second collection is found in Luke 16 (with the exception of vv. 16–18), which is framed by two parables: the crafty steward (16:1–9) and the poor man Lazarus (16:19–31). Jesus' sayings here on the right use of riches (16:10–15) are without parallel in Matthew (except v. 13; cf. Matt. 6:24).

Aside from these collections, one can read in eight different places in Luke texts related to the theme of poverty and sharing: loaning without any hope of return (6:34–35); generous unrestricted giving (6:38); the Pharisees redeeming themselves through almsgiving (11:41); inviting the poor for meals (14:13); the poor invited to the messianic banquet (14:21); renouncing all one's possessions to become a disciple (14:33); the story of Zacchaeus (19:1–10); the widow's mite (21:1–4). This last passage can also be found in Mark (12:41–44), the only Marcan text related to this theme, except for the Synoptic collection (10:17–22) as well as the passage on the "lure of riches" (Mark 4:19).

This simple alignment of texts already demonstrates the importance of the relationship to material goods in Luke's Gospel.

4. RADICALIZING THE LAW

Luke devotes an extensive section to the right use of riches. Matthew, desiring to propose an evangelical law, emphasizes its transcendence over the Mosaic Law—not that the latter is abrogated but, rather, deepened, led back to its roots, hence radicalized. The inaugural discourse of his Gospel (Matt. 5:1–7:27) brings together precisely everything concerning the transcendence of the old Law and concerning the sharper emphasis of its demands.

One reads, first of all, about the paradoxical blessings (or Beatitudes) addressed to all those who are in a situation of poverty, humility, need, suffering, or persecution and who, with a pure heart, seek to forgive and become peacemakers (5:3–12; the Lucan parallels: Luke 6:20–23).

Next is what are called the six antitheses. To the old teachings,

Jesus juxtaposes his own "radically other" demands: (1) not only is killing forbidden, but disciples should abstain from anger and abusive language and reconcile themselves as quickly as possible with their adversaries (only Matt. 5:21–26); (2) they must not only avoid adultery but all inner lust (Matt. 5:27–30); (3) divorce, formerly authorized, will no longer be so (Matt. 5:31–32); (4) all oath-taking is excluded (Matt. 5:33–37); (5) rather than taking vengeance, disciples must allow themselves to be abused, insulted, stripped, indicted, and exploited (Matt. 5:38–42); (6) following God's own example, they must love their enemies and pray for them (Matt. 5:43–48).

Disciples will also be asked not to judge or dwell upon the faults of others (Matt. 7:1–5). In a word, they must treat others as they would like to be treated (Matt. 7:12). The good things they do, such as almsgiving, prayer, and fasting, will be done before God alone and not paraded in front of others so as to be rewarded by them (Matt. 6:1–6, 16–18).

One sees that the road indicated is hard and the gate that leads to life narrow (Matt. 6:13–14). The demands are great and require a special effort.

These texts, with the exception of a few Lucan parallels that will be indicated when the discourse is analyzed, are generally peculiar to Matthew. Their arrangement serves to demonstrate Jesus' radicalization of the Law.

5. INDEPENDENT SAYINGS

The texts cited thus far are connected with collections of sayings built around certain concerns of the evangelists. We must now pick out certain sayings that are found outside of these collections or that appear in various other contexts.

First is the logion on the foot or eye that should be cut off or thrown away if it is a cause for scandal. This logion, used twice by Matthew in different contexts (Matt. 5:27–30: adultery; 18:8–9: scandal of the little ones), is also found in Mark (9:43–47: scandal of the little ones).

Second is the difficult saying on the kingdom of God being subjected to violence, and the violent taking it by storm (Matt. 11:12), which Matthew placed in a collection of sayings concerning John the Baptist (Matt. 11:2-19). Luke reports it outside of any context (16:16).

Finally, these brief and well-coined sentences are found in very different contexts: (1) the expression "the last will be first" can be read four times in the Synoptics—twice in Matthew (19:30: conclusion of the pericope on the promised reward; 20:16: conclusion of the parable on the vineyard laborers); once in Mark (10:31: same context as Matt. 19:30); once in Luke (13:30: conclusion of a diverse collection of sayings); (2) "He who is not with me is against me," common to Matthew and Luke (Matt. 12:30), follows in both cases the controversy over Beelzebul (Mark 3:22-27); (3) finally, there is the saying "Many are called but few are chosen," which only Matthew (22:14) associates with the double parable of the guests at the royal wedding feast and the guest without a wedding garment (Matt. 22:1-14).

Thus we have covered by a circular and repetitive process the totality of the Gospel sayings on radicality. This first approach ("logical" classification) provided a general but, I think, comprehensive view. Afterward, these sayings are grouped around certain points of interest—points or poles that form their original context.

PART TWO

TEXTUAL ANALYSIS

Until now we have simply cleared the ground and indicated the initial direction we wish to take. Except for a few indispensable observations, we have neither analyzed nor deepened the texts that we have taken and regrouped. Since this is the main purpose of our study, we must do so now.

We must, then, rapidly review the area covered in the section "Regrouping the Synoptic Sayings" in the preceding chapter. The texts already presented will be studied again. Using historical and literary criticism (historico-critical method), we must first see what the Gospel writers meant in each text (or group of texts). Even if only hypothesis, we shall try to perceive, whenever possible, the previous background of the text and the core of events or source sayings of which the text is a witness.

Indeed, our constant concern will be to highlight the radical dimensions and demands of the texts thus analyzed. Moreover, we shall try to determine for whom these demands are intended, both on the level of the Gospel redactors and from previous traditions.

After this analytical approach—a central part of our study— we shall be in a position to present an overview of the theme of radicalism, an overview based on a sober and fair analysis of the texts. Our purpose is to provide a close and detailed analysis, while at the same time avoiding the technical and scholarly apparatus to which many react negatively.

3

Radical Demands of Discipleship

As we have seen, a relatively important number of radical sayings are addressed to the disciples, those who shared Jesus' life and preaching. Before studying the radical traits found in their vocation narratives, their mission, and the instruction about their role as disciples, it will be useful to specify the Synoptics' use of the word "disciple" (*mathètès* in Greek).

DIFFERENT MEANINGS OF "DISCIPLE"

In Mark, when the word "disciple" is applied to those who follow Jesus, it always means the limited group of men, the twelve, whom Jesus chose as his companions and associated with his mission. Mark uses both designations ("disciple" and "the twelve") without distinction, while assuming the existence of a larger circle around Jesus (Mark 3:34; 4:10,32; 15:40). Matthew, though following Mark, utilizes at least once the expression "disciple" in its Christian meaning of "believer in Jesus" (Matt. 10:42; cf. also 28:18).

Luke, on the other hand, makes a clear distinction between the twelve and a larger group of disciples. Such is the case for the election of the twelve who are chosen from among the disciples whom Jesus calls (Luke 6:13). These disciples make up "a large gathering" (Luke 6:17; 19:37); women are included (Luke 8:1-3); Jesus sends seventy-two of them on mission (Luke 10:1). Later, in the Acts of the Apostles, the word "disciple" no longer designates the ones who accompanied the earthly Jesus in his life and mission but those who have faith in the risen Lord and have become members of the believing community (Acts 6:1; 2:7; 9:26).

A parallel meaning can be found in John's Gospel. Alongside the narrow use of the word (a disciple is one who shares Jesus' earthly life: John 2:2; 3:22; 6:3), John uses the same term for those who believe in Jesus and who love their neighbor, namely, believing Christians (for example, see John 8:31; 13:35).[1]

In our study, the word will be used in both accepted forms. In this chapter—beginning with the title—the word maintains its narrow meaning: a man who was part of the chosen group around Jesus. Elsewhere, unless otherwise indicated, it will carry the wider meaning of Christian believer.

THE CALL TO DISCIPLESHIP AND RADICALISM

There are various narratives on the vocation to follow Jesus in the Synoptic Gospels. Some of these narratives describe well-known personalities: Peter and Andrew, James and John, Levi. Others maintain the disciple's anonymity. It is true that the latter are callings that are unsuccessful. We shall study these two types of callings by focusing not on the structure of the narratives or their purpose (to follow Jesus) but, in accordance with our goal, on the radical demands that they exemplify.

1. PERSONAL VOCATIONS

Jesus' first disciples are called to follow him when he passes by the lake of Galilee. Seeing two fishermen, Simon and Andrew, casting their nets in the water, Jesus calls them to follow him and become "fishers of men." "Immediately leaving their nets, they followed him" (Mark 1:16–18). A little farther on the same scene is repeated for "James son of Zebedee and his brother John" who, mending their nets in the company of their father and his employees, leave "their father Zebedee in the boat with the men he employed" (Mark 1:19–20).

Mark and Matthew agree almost word for word. Luke's narrative (5:1–11), though situated in a very different context (Jesus in Peter's boat; the miraculous catch of fish), does not mention Andrew but does present parallels: Peter is called to "catch men" (Luke 5:10); James and John, "bringing their boats back to land, . . . left everything" and followed Jesus (Luke 5:11).

Jesus' initiative and demands must be emphasized in these narratives devoted exclusively to the call: "Follow me and I will make you into fishers of men" (Mark 1:18). This is all Jesus requires. The narrators are the ones who point out the disciples' immediate obedience and various abandonments. They leave their nets, boats, employees (their trade: Mark 1:18-20), as well as their father (their family: Mark 1:20). Luke, without going into detail, merely says (and not for the last time) "they left everything" (Luke 5:11).

Levi's vocation (Mark 2:13-14) is described according to the same schema: Jesus' initiative, the call to follow, the immediate response. Mark and Matthew, after noting Levi's trade ("sitting by the customs house"), say nothing of his abandonments (obviously implied). Luke, however, further specifies that "leaving everything, he got up and followed him" (Luke 5:28). Still, that does not prevent Levi from afterward having a great reception for "a large gathering of tax collectors and others" (Luke 5:29). Mark and Matthew specify "sinners" (Mark 2:15).

This analysis demonstrates that although the narratives center on Jesus' sovereign call inviting others to join him, the narrators (especially Luke) always mention, aside from the immediate response, the practical consequence: a break either with one's family or with one's trade. One cannot, however, speak of ascetic detachment or poverty. In joining Jesus, one radically changes one's lifestyle and trade, not out of scorn for material goods or family but because a different kind of existence imposes itself.

Each narrative understandably carries a distinctive imprint (especially strong in Luke) of the evangelist who wrote it. The miraculous catch of fish, which serves as a framework for the vocation of the first disciples (Luke 5:1-3), has points in common with the post-resurrection miraculous catch of fish (John 21:1-14). Moreover, Luke emphasizes the act of leaving everything: "They left everything" (*panta*). Although a similar literary schema can be found in the narrative of Elijah's call of Elisah (1 Kings 19:19-21), and although one can imagine a duplicated construction of accounts (Peter and Andrew's vocations next to James and John's), the basic historical fact, nevertheless, remains undeniable. Those called to follow Jesus severed ties with their life-and work-settings, in order to be with him. This was noted by those who transcribed and those who heard the accounts in the primitive Christian community.

2. ABSOLUTE DEMANDS

Although personal vocations are reported in all three traditions, Luke and Matthew (the double tradition) share in common a small group of sayings on the demands of the disciple's vocation (Matt. 8:18–22). No specific person is mentioned; anonymity is maintained: "someone," "another" (Luke), "a scribe," "another disciple" (Matthew). Where these unknown personalities come from or how they respond to the challenge is not disclosed. They are there to illustrate the unparalleled demands imposed on Jesus' followers.

The first two demands are common to both evangelists. Someone ("a scribe," Matthew specifies, 8:19) manifests to Jesus his desire to follow him "wherever you go." Here it is not Jesus who calls but, rather, a man who addresses himself, hoping for a call or a confirmation. Jesus' response is far from inviting. He is itinerant, has less of a home than foxes or birds of the air, and never even knows where he will spend the night. Whoever plans to follow him should weigh well the cost and be ready for complete uprootedness and daily insecurity.

The second example is presented differently by the two evangelists. In Luke it is Jesus who calls someone to follow him (Luke 9:59). That person asks permission first to go bury his deceased father. Jesus responds with a hard and almost scornful paradox: "Leave the dead to bury their dead; your duty is to go and spread the news of the kingdom of God" (Luke 9:60). Even the demands of the Law (which is the will of God!) must yield before Jesus' demands and the urgency of the call. The most sacred duties toward parents are of no account when it is a matter of following Jesus.

In Matthew it is "one of his disciples" who asks Jesus for permission to bury his father (Matt. 8:21). Jesus answers: "Follow me, and leave the dead to bury their dead" (Matt. 8:22). Although the basic meaning is the same, there is nonetheless a slight difference. One is given the impression that the man in Matthew's account is not so much a historical "prospective" disciple (as in Luke) but a "Christian" disciple being reminded that "following Jesus" must prevail over the most deeply rooted feelings and duties. In proposing such a demand, Jesus places his and the disciple's mission above all other human plans or demands imposed by God.[2]

The last case (peculiar to Luke 9:61-62) once again involves an unknown, "another" (Luke 9:61), who offers himself as a disciple but asks permission first to take leave of his own people. Just as before, Jesus reminds him that once the commitment is made and "the hand laid on the plow," one must no longer look back; otherwise one is unfit for the kingdom of God (Luke 9:62). The teaching is the same: one must make an absolute commitment without regrets or afterthoughts, and nothing must take preference over following Jesus.

Even though there are allusions to specific breaks, these three examples (living without a roof over one's head, severing ties with one's own people, neglecting even the final duties toward one's parents) have in fact a single emphasis. To be with Jesus, to be his disciple, to follow him, one must be ready for everything and prefer him over everything. The two areas indicated (severing ties with one's family, itinerant insecurity) illustrate this all-encompassing demand. The collection of sayings we have studied is not intended to demand some concrete renunciation but to affirm the unconditional and central character of the commitment to follow Jesus, which takes priority over all other values.

INSTRUCTIONS FOR THE DISCIPLES SENT ON MISSION

Jesus' disciples are sent to the Jews (only Matt. 10:5-6). This mission, narrated by the Synoptics (Mark 6:7-13), is contained in Matthew's "missionary" or "apostolic" discourse (Matt. 10:1-42). Here the evangelist regroups various sayings concerning the fate the disciple can expect, particularly: family opposition (Matt. 10:34-36), hate, persecutions, and even death (Matt. 10:17-24). Luke repeats the mission narrative in almost identical terms in the mission of the seventy-two (Luke 10:1-12).

This double series of texts—the mission of the twelve in Matthew's discourse and the mission of the seventy-two in Luke—entails important radical demands, which we must now analyze.

1. PROVISIONS FOR MISSION

Sent out in pairs (Mark 6:7; Luke 10:1) to proclaim the coming of the kingdom and bring healing (Matt. 10:7), invested with authority over unclean spirits (Mark 6:7), the twelve receive particularly strict instructions concerning their baggage and provisions. They are forbidden to bring bread, haversack, copper for their purses, or to wear two tunics (Mark 6:8-9). Matthew and Luke add that having a staff is prohibited (Matt. 10:10). Matthew alone still excludes sandals (Matt. 10:10). Strangely enough, Mark authorizes both staff and sandals (Mark 6:8-9), though, like Luke, he begins the instructions with the absolute requirement: "take nothing for the journey" (Mark 6:8).

The instructions given to the seventy-two (Luke 10:1-2) prohibit purse and haversack, as well as sandals. And when, during the Last Supper, Jesus speaks of the mission of the twelve (Luke 22:35-38), he enumerates not the objects forbidden to the twelve (staff, haversack, bread, money, two tunics: Luke 9:3) but those forbidden to the seventy-two: purse, haversack, sandals.

What conclusion can we draw from this initial analysis? On the literary level, one might suppose that before the evangelists' final redaction, two very similar mission narratives existed. Luke retained both and applied one of them to the seventy-two. Matthew avoided what seemed to him a repetition, though still inserting in his missionary discourse: "the workman deserves his keep" (Matt. 10:10b; Luke 10:7b) and "If the house deserves it, let your peace descend upon it" (Matt. 10:13; Luke 10:6). As for the recommendations themselves, two points need clarification: the specific object of these recommendations and their meaning.

Forbidden Objects

The only constant in both discourses is the prohibition of the haversack (*pèra* in Greek). This is the case in the triple tradition (Mark 6:8) as well as in Luke (10:4). Money in its various forms (gold: only Matthew; silver: Matthew and Luke; copper: Matthew and Luke) and taking two tunics are forbidden in the first discourse but not in the second. Sandals, excluded in Matthew (10:10) and in Luke's second discourse, are explicitly allowed by Mark (6:9). Mark and Luke forbid bringing bread (Mark 6:8; Luke 9:3); Matthew and Luke forbid the staff (Matt. 10:10; Luke 9:3), while Mark authorizes it (Mark 6:8). Finally, Luke alone, in the second discourse, forbids a purse (*ballantion,* Luke 10:4).

We can derive two observations from this accumulation of details: (1) originally, the historical mission to the Jews seemed to have entailed the interdict of money and provisions, and most likely also of useful equipment for the journey: sandals and staff; (2) the variant lists, as well as the fact that Mark authorized what others forbade, indicates the freedom taken with the tradition when adapting the Lord's sayings to concrete situations.

Meaning of the Interdicts

What is the meaning of these interdicts? Can we simply speak, as is often done, of poverty of missionaries? Are we talking about ascetical poverty (scorn for wealth) or a poverty in function of mission (disinterestedness of the missionary for the sake of edifying)?

The context of both discourses orients us in a different direction. This context appears clearly in Luke's second discourse, as well as in Matthew, the latter drawing inspiration from the former. It is primarily the urgency of the message that requires the messenger not to greet anyone along the way. We would even be tempted to connect this demand for traveling light with the absence of a second tunic, sandals, and staff. Luke and Matthew strongly emphasize the idea (also present in Mark) that "the laborer deserves his wages" or his "food and drink" (Luke 10:7; Matt. 10:10) and that one should stay in the same house where one is welcomed and fed (Luke 10:7). The three traditions, it is true, do not say why one must stay in the same house, but everything leads us to believe that the motive or reason is the same as in Luke: to eat and drink what they offer (Luke 10:7; cf. also Luke 22:35).

Thus it is because the ones sent will be welcomed and nourished by the believing hearers of the Word that they are not to take money or provisions (haversack, bread). The mission requires speed, traveling light, freedom. The rest, which is secondary to the mission, the disciples will not lack; they are not to be concerned or encumbered with it. God and the goodwill of the hearers will provide. The ones sent are like a peaceful army who invade a country, live at the expense of its inhabitants, and are not "short of anything" (Luke 22:35). It is true, however, that once the conditions change and the disciples are not sure of being received, different behavior is necessary and both purse and haversack are required (Luke 22:36).

Something needs to be said about the potential meaning of the prohibited staff and sandals. The oddity of this interdict as well as the fact that it is found in the earliest traditions tends to make us believe that the data here do not come from the tradition but from Jesus himself.[3] What, then, does this interdict mean? One could assume that it is meant to facilitate the speed and ease of the journey, but then the contrary would be expected for staff and sandals, which, rather than inhibiting the journey, facilitate it. Some exegetes propose symbolic meanings: such behavior would emphasize the holiness of the mission. As a matter of fact, a talmudic text requires that those who climb to the Temple in Jerusalem do so barefoot, without staff or purse. The instruction would then mean "in your mission, you must present yourselves like those who stand before the holiness of God."[4] By removing this interdict (why emphasize taking a staff and wearing sandals when, for a traveler, this is taken for granted?) and in allowing for normal practice, Mark may have been alluding to Exodus 12:11, which prescribes eating the paschal lamb "with a girdle around your waist, sandals on your feet, a staff in your hand" in order to be ready for the road.[5]

2. THE FATE OF THE MISSIONARY

During their mission as witnesses, the disciples can expect violent opposition from the hands of the religious and civil authorities of their time (Mark 13:9); and even more, their own family members will rise up against them (Mark 13:12).

Initially it will be the religious authorities who will attack them. They will seize missionaries, persecute them (Luke 21:12), and hand them over to the Sanhedrin. The missionaries will be beaten in the synagogues and, finally, they will be brought before kings and governors (Mark 13:9). The final verdict is terrible: "you will be hated by all" (Mark 13:13).

Indeed, even the family will oppose itself to the missionaries: "Brother will betray brother to death, and the father his child; children will rise against their parents and have them put to death" (Mark 13:12; Matt. 10:21). Luke makes this even more personal: "You will be betrayed even by parents and brothers, relations and friends; and some of you will be put to death" (Luke 21:16).

One notices that the idea of being put to death is closely related to family opposition. Death is not explicitly mentioned for persecutions from the synagogue.

The anomaly, the horror of these family divisions (the cause of which is Jesus' coming) are emphasized by another text of the double tradition: "Do not suppose that I have come to bring peace to the earth; it is not peace I have come to bring, but a sword. For I have come to set a man against his father, a daughter against her mother, a daughter-in-law against her mother-in-law. A man's enemies will be those of his own household" (Matt. 10:34–36, quoting Mic. 7:6).

In Mark and Luke the texts on hate and persecutions unto death are part of the eschatological discourse addressed to the twelve (Mark 13:9, 11–13; Luke 21:12, 16, 17). Matthew inserts them in the missionary discourse, also addressed to the twelve, to announce what the missionaries can expect in their task (Matt. 10:17–18, 21–22). Also in his version of the eschatological discourse, Matthew omits these texts and simply summarizes them: "They will hand you over to be tortured and put to death; and you will be hated by all the nations" (Matt. 24:9).

The text on Jesus as cause of these family divisions is found in the missionary discourse (Matt. 10:21–22), while Luke presents it in no special context (Luke 12:51–53).

Jesus' sayings on the suffering that the missionaries can expect have, to be sure, a prophetic tone. This clearly was the condition of many disciples in the first decades of the Christian mission in Jewish quarters as well as before Roman tribunals. This was not the case, however, when Jesus was alive (Luke 22:35). Undeniably, the situation in which the early Christians lived colored and shaped *ex eventu* the descriptions of the Gospels.

A question arises: Did Jesus foresee and predict what awaited the twelve, as well as the first Christian missionaries? In other words, do the sayings about coming persecutions and death express only the experience of the primitive community, or does the core go back to Jesus himself? The answer to such a question (which repeatedly arises in the course of this study) is linked to a decision on a preliminary position. For those who believe that Jesus had a global awareness of his mission, that he intuitively glimpsed the "failure" of his death, and that he nonetheless foresaw a future to the work he had begun (in the image of his own fate), the answer will be a positive one. In a way no doubt less clear than the texts indicate, the disciples were forewarned on what they could expect, for "the disciple is not superior to his teacher, nor the slave to his master" (Matt. 10:24). The same saying is found in John 13:16; 15:20 and Luke 6:40 (but in the latter, the meaning is less clear).

Thus the disciple is to be confronted by brutal opposition, even leading to death: "If they have called the master of the household Beelzebul, what will they not say of his household?" (only Matt. 10:25). This pertains dramatically to those in close association as well as those in the larger circle; hostility, not hospitality, is promised.

THE LEAST AND THE GREATEST

The twelve enjoyed privileged positions at Jesus' side. In the Gospel tradition, Jesus promises that they will share his kingship and his function as judge; they will sit on twelve thrones and judge the twelve tribes of Israel (Matt. 19:28). They will sit and eat at this table in the kingdom because they stood faithfully by him in his trials (Luke 22:28–30).

But the same tradition, with an even greater emphasis, echoes the far too worldly ambitions of the disciples and Jesus' warnings against the snare of the will to power.

1. SYNOPTIC SAYINGS

The collection of Synoptic sayings teach that humility and service are required of those who think that they hold the first places.

This theme is twice linked with the child episode: the quarrel of the disciples about who is the greatest (Mark 9:33-37); the scene with the children (Mark 10:13-16). A third episode, at least in Matthew and Mark, describes the sons of Zebedee desiring to occupy the first places (Mark 10:41-45; Luke 22:24-30, in another context). All these pericopes repeatedly affirm: the first must become like a slave and the greatest must become the least.

In the first episode the disciples ask themselves who among them is the greatest (Mark 9:33-37). Jesus' direct and paradoxical response about welcoming children squelches this drive for power. The explicit verse in Luke reads:"The least among you all, that is the one who is great" (9:48c), and in Matthew, verse 3 and especially 4: "unless you turn and become like children, you will never enter the kingdom of heaven. Whoever humbles himself like this child, he is the greatest in the kingdom of heaven" (Matt. 18:3-4, RSV). The verse is less clear in Mark: "If anyone wants to be first, he must make himself last of all and the servant of all" (9:35).

Matthew's verses relate the dispute of who is the greatest to the presence of the child. In Mark and Luke, on the other hand, the two narratives are not harmonized and the sayings on the child seem to have no direct bearing on the quarrel.

Thus this first episode seems to juxtapose (clearly in Mark, with successful attempts to harmonize them in Matthew, less successful ones in Luke) two logia (pronouncement stories) from different sources: one on humility and service (Mark 9:35); the other on welcoming little ones (Mark 9:37). It is difficult to determine to which of these two logia the scene of the child is originally linked.

The second episode is less composite. We see the disciples scolding those who are bringing children to Jesus (Mark 10:13-16). But Jesus welcomes the little ones and, on this occasion, pronounces a saying identical in all three traditions: "For it is to such as these that the kingdom of God belongs" (Mark 10:14b). Mark and Luke continue, "I tell you solemnly, anyone who does not welcome the kingdom of God like a little child will never enter it" (Mark 10:15).

If this last sentence is omitted by Matthew, it is because for him an equivalent meaning can be found in the preceding episode. Thus it is little children, with their attitude of humility and weakness and their need and powerlessness, who are proposed to the disciples and all hearers of the gospel as an example of how to receive the good news. Previously the little child served as model to the disciples in their exercise of authority (the great must become like little children). Now the child is the image of need, weakness, and, by the same token, of the availability and openness required of every believing disciple.[6]

The third pericope (Mark 10:35-45 and Matt. 20:20-28 only) relates the request of the sons of Zebedee (Mark; or of their mother: Matthew) to occupy the first place next to Jesus in his glory. After the sayings on the sharing of the cup (the Passion), which Jesus predicts to the two disciples, and before the indignant reaction of the ten others, Jesus describes the proper behavior of those who occupy the first places in his community. In earthly kingdoms the claimants of power exercise it despotically, and the great make their authority felt. "This is not to happen among you. No; anyone who wants to become great among you must be your servant, and anyone who wants to be first among you must be slave to all" (Mark 10:42-44).

Although Luke has not preserved the episode of the sons of Zebedee, he nonetheless gives the same teaching in the framework of the Last Supper (Luke 22:24-27). To the debate about who among them is the greatest (parallel in context to the first episode: Mark 9:33), Jesus responds with sayings almost identical to those that have just been presented. Only the details are different: it is the rulers of peoples who dominate others and require honorary titles for themselves (benefactors: *evergetai*). In Mark and Matthew, the opposition is between great/servant, first/slave; Luke opposes greatest/youngest (*neôteros*), leader (*égoumenos*)/ servant (*diakonos*). These last two words seem to be technical terms used in the first primitive Christian communities to designate those invested with specific functions (cf. Acts 5:6: *neôteros*; 15:22: *égoumenos*).

This teaching ends in Mark and Matthew by a reminder that Jesus "did not come to be served but to serve, and to give his life as a ransom for many" (Mark 10:45). Luke situates these same instructions in the framework of a meal: "For which is the greater, one who sits at table or one who serves? Is it not the one who sits at table? But I am among you as one who serves [*diakonon*]'' (Luke 22:27, RSV).

2. MATTHEW AND LUKE

To these three Synoptic texts we must add two others, one from Matthew and the other from Luke, related to the present theme.

In Matthew's great polemic against the scribes and the Pharisees (Matt. 23:1–36), a polemic that has a few parallels in Mark (12:38–40) and a few more in Luke (20:45–47; 11:39–52), Jesus criticizes the ambition and the ostentation of these men. They desire places of honor at table, front seats in the synagogues, greetings in the street, titles such as Rabbi (Matt. 23:6–7). To the crowds who are listening to him and to the disciples, Jesus says (Matt. 23:8–12):

8 You, however, must not allow yourselves to be called Rabbi, since you have only one Master, and you are all brothers.

9 You must call no one on earth your father, since you have only one Father, and he is in heaven.

10 Nor must you allow yourselves to be called teachers, for you have only one Teacher, the Christ.

11 The greatest among you must be your servant.

12 Anyone who exalts himself will be humbled, and anyone who humbles himself will be exalted.

This passage has no parallel in Mark or Luke, but similar declarations are attributed by John to Jesus washing the feet of his disciples (John 13:12–17). It is evident that the three verses (8–10), when examined according to our logical approach, present some confusion. ''You are all brothers,'' would fit better after verse 9: ''You must call no one on earth your father. . . .'' Verses 8 to 10 seem to be doublets, since the words ''master'' (*didaskalos*) and ''teacher'' (*kathègètès*) carry the same meaning. The total picture bears the obvious imprint of the community; nothing, however, prevents us from thinking that warnings of this type could have been given, in one form or another, by Jesus himself. Matthew has regrouped them, with some repetition, and applied them to specific situations of the primitive community.

According to Jewish custom scribes did indeed receive honorary titles. The title Rabbi (from *rab*, "great") meant something like Your Excellency or My Lord; it became synonymous to Master-Teacher. The name Father was likewise applied to important religious personalities. The greatest masters of the time, Hillel and Shammai (first century), were called Fathers of the World. Guide or Teacher (*kathègètès*) was also an honorary title.[7] These names corresponded to a custom but also expressed the truth of certain human situations: there did exist fathers and sons, lords and servants, masters and disciples. Jesus refuses this structure. In his community, there will no longer be a master, a father, or a teacher other than God and Jesus. The disciples' relationships among themselves can only be fraternal ones: "you are all brothers" (Matt. 23:8).

Let us note here that the proverb of verse 12 ("Anyone who exalts himself will be humbled") is presented with the preceding verse ("The greatest among you must be your servant") as a conclusion to the teachings on the refusal of titles. We shall return to verse 11, already encountered previously. The proverb "Anyone who exalts himself will be humbled" can be found in four different contexts in Matthew/Luke (Matt. 18:4; 23:12; Luke 14:11; 18:14). In addition to using it in the pericope studied here, Matthew uses it in a modified form in the dispute on who is the greatest (Matt. 18:1–5): "Whoever humbles himself like this child, he is the greatest in the kingdom of heaven" (RSV).

Luke presents it in an identical form as a conclusion: "Everyone who exalts himself will be humbled." It appears once in the parable of choosing places at the table: "Make your way to the lowest place . . . so that when your host comes, he may say, 'My friend, move up higher' " (Luke 14:7–11). The other episode, of the Pharisee and the publican (Luke 18:9–14), is an invitation to choose the lowest place whatever the circumstances. This saying seems to have been used often, if not by Jesus at least by the gospel tradition.

These sayings, which urge a complete reversal of situations (the first must become last; the greatest, the least; the leader, servant), are used twice by each of the Synoptics. The same demand is made six times (Mark 9:35; 10:43–44; Matt. 20:26; 23:11; Luke 9:48; 22:26). This once again demonstrates the impact this saying had on the narrators and auditors of the gospel.

SYNTHESIS OF THE RADICALISM OF DISCIPLESHIP

Now that we have finished our examination of the texts, let us try to synthesize the various issues raised: the peculiarities in the Synoptic presentations, the content of the demands, those for whom they are intended, and their motivations.

1. PECULIARITIES IN THE SYNOPTICS

Most of the texts examined in this chapter are derived from the triple tradition. The exceptions are the passage on the demands of the vocation (Matt. 8:18–22), common to Matthew/Luke, and a text peculiar to Matthew (refusal of titles). To be noted again in Luke is the radical abandonment of everything. Also to be noted is that the narrative on who is the greatest (Mark 9:33–37) and the request of the sons of Zebedee (Mark 10:35–45) follow, respectively, the second and third predictions of the Passion in the Synoptics. (Luke, however, has not preserved the episode of the sons of Zebedee.) This literary bond, certainly very old, shows how the theme of the disciple and his or her behavior was originally associated with the idea of the Passion. Far from claiming privileges for themselves, disciples must be ready to share the fate of the master. Between this fate and the ambition of the disciples is a glaring contrast.

2. THE DEMANDS

Jesus' call initiates all the demands. After this call no hesitation, no looking back is allowed. In responding to it, one must prepare for material insecurity, rejection, persecution, hate, and even death. The ties with one's family and one's trade are broken. Luke, moreover, insists on the necessity of leaving *everything* (Luke 5:11, 28).

It is when the disciples are sent on mission that more detailed prescriptions are given on what must be left behind (and on this point one must follow Mark). These are the only Gospel texts that specify the use of things and material poverty: no money, bread, haversack, change of clothes, sandals, or staff. The meaning of this divestiture is not so easy to grasp as it may seem. Perhaps, in fact, there are many meanings.

The people in question are those who hold a special position in the community. They are required to feel and behave as the least—that is, like little children and slaves—and to refuse honorary places and titles.

3. THE RECIPIENTS OF THE TEXTS

Since the texts that we have analyzed concern "disciples" in the narrow meaning of the word, the radical demands should be reserved for them. But it is not that clear. The narratives of personal vocation (Peter and Andrew, James and John, Levi) bring to the forefront specific historical figures. However, the conditions proposed to anonymous prospective disciples from among "the great crowds" (Matt. 8:18) surrounding Jesus on "the road for Jerusalem" (Luke 9:51–57) do not seem limited to a restricted group. In addition to these concrete historical examples, every eventual disciple, every believer in Jesus, is singled out and warned of the cost of following Jesus.

Likewise the call to mission and the prediction of persecutions do not, strictly speaking, concern only the twelve (or the seventy-two). In fact, in examining closely these texts one sees that they apply as gospels to the missionaries of the community (Matthew's missionary discourse) and even to all persecuted believers. Some redactors thus emphasize that Jesus' instructions retain their validity in circumstances other than those of the immediate disciples.

The warnings against the will to power (disputes on being first) are addressed to those who hold positions of authority in the community. To be sure, these are first of all the twelve, but here again the exhortations are extended. The child, proposed first of all as an example of humility to ambitious disciples (only Matt. 18:3), in another episode becomes the model for all believers of how to receive the kingdom (Mark 10:15; Luke 18:17). The recommendation to refuse honorary titles (also pronounced before the crowd and the disciples: Matt. 23:1), uses an undefined "you" (Matt. 23:8)—meaning not only the twelve but the listening crowd and, ultimately, all those whom Jesus' words reach.

4. MOTIVATIONS OF RADICALISM

The theme of discipleship around which the texts revolve correlates to the theme of master. It is because one is called to "be with Jesus" (this expression in Mark 3:14 means the twelve; cf. also Mark 5:18) that everything else has meaning and becomes possible. At the center of all the texts is the sharply focused presence of Jesus and his call. Jesus fills the entire space, which explains why the most vital realities of the person (family bonds, work, security, self-affirmation) are seemingly pulverized and thrust into the background. Thus the texts analyzed insist less on required behavior—in fact, this is mentioned only in passing, as a consequence—than on the root of the decisions. And this root is the centrality of Jesus for whom and by whom all choices are made. It is also, secondarily, the urgency of mission. But behind all the narratives and all the demands, one can detect the profile of Jesus, who calls and serves as model.

NOTES

1. A detailed presentation of this question appears in H. J. Degenhardt, *Lukas—Evangelist der Armen* (Stuttgart: Kath. Bibelwerk, 1965), pp. 27–28; J. Dupont, "Renoncer à tous ses biens," *Nouvelle Revue Théologique* 93 (1971): 563–82 (esp. pp. 577–79); A. Schulz, *Nachfolgen und Nachahme* (Munich: Kösel, 1962), pp. 48–49, 137–40.

2. M. Hengel, *Nachfolge und Charisma* (Berlin: Töpelmann, 1968), basically concerned with analyzing the Matt. 8:21–22 passage, does a good job of emphasizing Jesus' sovereign authority.

3. In the same vein, E. Percy, *Die Botschaft Jesu* (Lund: C. W. K. Gleerup, 1953), pp. 29–30. Such is not the opinion of Bultmann, *Die Geschichte der synoptischen Tradition* (Göttingen: Vandenhoeck

and Ruprecht, 1967), p. 155, nor of Braun, *Spätjüdisch—häretischer und frühchristlicher Radikalismus*, 2 vols. (Tübingen: J. C. B. Mohr, 1969), 2:76, n. 1, who tend toward a creation by the community.

4. Text quoted by Percy, *Die Botschaft*, p. 130. The same position is upheld by T. W. Manson, *The Sayings of Jesus* (London: SCM Press, 1971), p. 181.

5. Opinion of M. E. Boismard, *Synopse des quatre évangiles en français*, 2 vols. (Paris: Cerf, 1972), 2:216.

6. On the theme of the child, see the exhaustive study by S. Légasse, *Jésus et l'enfant,* Études Bibliques (Paris: Gabalda, 1969).

7. See G. Vermes, *Jesus the Jew* (New York: Macmillan, 1974), p. 115; Manson, *Sayings,* pp. 231-32.

4

Sayings on Renunciation

Jesus' most radical sayings have been retained and reassembled in very distinctive collections by both the triple and the double traditions. Surprisingly, some of them have an almost literal Johannine equivalent.

The first collection, which the Synoptics hold in common (Mark 8:34–9:1), is noted by its context. In the three Gospels, it is set in an almost identical series of events and words: Peter's confession, the first prediction of the Passion, the collection on renunciation, the Transfiguration. To preserve such a sequence without modifying it (a rather rare occurrence), there must have existed a solid center, a core idea that no redactor dared to touch. This proves, if not the antiquity of the collection, at least the link between events that seemed necessary and untouchable.

The second collection (the double tradition: Matt. 10:37–39) is set in different contexts. Matthew inserts it in his missionary discourse, addressed in principle to the twelve. In Luke it appears in his great narrative of the "ascent to Jerusalem" (9:51–19:27), in a series of apparently unconnected teachings.

Finally, in relationship to these two collections we shall examine the text, peculiar to Matthew, on the eunuchs (Matt. 19:10–12).

SYNOPTIC COLLECTION: TO DENY ONESELF AND TAKE UP ONE'S CROSS (MARK 8:34–9:1)

In his confession (Mark 8:27–30) Peter, the foremost of the disciples, acknowledges the unique character of the person and mission of Jesus whom he affirms as Messiah (all three traditions) and as the Son of God (only Matt.). His confession is followed by the first prediction of the Passion. Jesus predicts his rejection by the religious leaders, his sufferings, his death, and his rising from the dead (Mark 8:31).On this point Peter intervenes to persuade him otherwise and Jesus responds by rebuking him (Mark 8: 32–33; Luke does not mention this rebuff).

This is when the declaration about the cross appears. According to Mark, Jesus speaks to the disciples and the crowd (Mark 8:34). Luke generalizes by writing "to all he said" (Luke 9:23). In Matthew only the disciples hear the declaration.

This episode in Mark is composed of six distinct logia; Matthew and Luke keep only five. Let us examine each one.

1. ANALYSIS

a. The first saying is identical word for word in Mark/Matthew (Mark 8:34) with minor variants in Luke: "If anyone wants to be a follower of mine,[1] let him renounce himself and take up his cross [Luke adds "every day"] and follow me." We find the same (slightly modified) saying two other times (Matt. 10:38; Luke 14:27). Thus the gospel tradition will have repeated it five times.

The expressions "to come after," "to come behind" (*erchesthai opiso*), and "to follow" (*akolouthein*) are almost equivalent and indicate the action of becoming Jesus' disciple, sharing his life and mission. Their repetition at the beginning and end of the sentence is somewhat of a tautology. To begin following Jesus, to join the group of disciples (we see here to what extent, for in Mark and Luke the idea is broadened: all believers seem capable of doing so), two conditions are necessary: deny oneself and take up one's cross (Luke: daily).

In relating to another person, to deny him or her means not to acknowledge that person, not to take that person into account, to detach oneself from whatever bonds there are. That is how Peter denies Jesus (Mark 14:30, 69, 70). To deny oneself is to fail to take into account what is deepest in oneself: the desire for self-affirmation and life.

In the post-Easter perspective, to take up one's cross obviously evokes a series of events related with Jesus' Passion and death, such as Simon of Cyrene carrying Jesus' cross to the hill where he died (Mark 15:21; John says that Jesus himself carried his cross: John 19:17). According to this perspective, to take up one's cross would mean to be ready to share Jesus' fate, even a death like his. Luke's insertion, "every day" would mean to bear throughout one's life the difficulties of being a Christian and to live in conformity with Jesus' demands.

Does this imply that the saying, especially the image of taking up one's cross, originates *post eventum* in the community? Nothing here leads us to make such a hypothesis. Even if one hesitates to see the saying as Jesus' direct prediction of his death on the cross and his announcement that sharing this fate is required of the disciple (would such a prediction at that time have meant anything to the disciples?), other interpretations, which limit the origin of the saying to Jesus, remain possible.

The most likely interpretation sees the cross not primarily as Jesus' cross but as an allusion to enduring the most cruel death known to the ancient world. It would be a traditional image (in particular, for the Zealot resisters contemporary to Jesus) of the suffering and sacrifice of self.[2]

The original meaning, then, of this saying would be as follows: whoever becomes Jesus' disciple must expect eventual death (and what a death!). To prepare for this death, one must forget oneself, lose oneself, and deny oneself rather than holding onto one's life. To go behind Jesus, to follow him, leads to this point, as eloquently expressed in the Passion prediction.

b. The second saying (Mark 8:35) can also be found in three other places (Matt. 10:39; Luke 17:33; John 12:25). Thus it is quoted six times in the Gospels. As with the preceding saying its wording is also identical in each Synoptic account: "For anyone who wants to save his life will lose it; but anyone who loses his life for my sake, and for the sake of the gospel, will save it." In John's Gospel (the only example of a saying of Jesus which he has in common with the Synoptics), it reads as follows (John 12:25): "Anyone who loves his life loses it; anyone who hates [instead of "loses"] his life in this world will keep it for the eternal life."

The particle "for" (*gar*) connects this text with the preceding saying. To deny oneself and take up one's cross is, indeed, to consent and, even more, to contribute to one's own loss (in Greek, the verb "to lose" is active). Paradoxically, refusing to deny oneself, seeking to save oneself or spare one's life (*psyche* here equals life or simply one's personhood) really leads to the loss of one's life. But the one who hands over his or her life preserves it. Matthew accentuates the paradox by opposing the words "lose" and "find": the one who loses, finds. The paradox, nonetheless, is not a play on words. John explains in his Gospel: "Anyone who loves [replacing "seeks to save"] his life loses it; anyone who hates [instead of "loses"] his life in this world will keep it for the eternal life" (John 12:25). There are two lives and two selves: one, an existence in history, rooted in time and space, protected by the instinct of preservation and survival; the other, a different type of existence linked to the world of God, of Jesus, open to what is to come: "eternal life." To enter into this second existence one must not hesitate to sacrifice the first.

This sacrifice is not required gratuitously or as a flight from life. It is for Jesus' sake that one must learn to lose one's life. Mark makes this more explicit (perhaps under some Pauline influences) by adding "for the sake of the gospel" (Mark 8:35; the same expression: Mark 10:29). The loss of one's life has meaning only in relationship to Jesus, whom one has chosen and in whose fate one participates. Faith in the gospel and its proclamation to men and women exposes the disciple (as it especially did the first Christian generation) to this risk. One loses oneself "for the sake of the gospel" when one accepts the death to which its preaching can lead. Thus we see that the two sayings, even if they may have originally been independent of each other, draw together. By different images and emphases they convey the same demand: the one who joins Jesus must be ready for martyrdom. A more moralistic addition emerges in Luke (9:23): one loses oneself when one daily accepts to live for others.

c. The third logion (Mark 8:36), common to all, appears in quite different versions, but the meaning is not affected. Let us read it as found in Mark, while indicating the Lucan variants: "What gain, then, is it for a man to win the whole world and ruin his life [Luke: to have lost or ruined his very self]?"

The logical continuity with what has preceded is readily apparent through the word "lost" (Luke), or its equivalent "ruin," and likewise the permanency of the Matthew/Marcan expression "life" (*psyche*). But let us acknowledge that, in spite of the connection desired by the redactors (the particle *gar* introduces each of the first five logia), the unity of meaning is not immediately obvious. The sentence, a kind of proverb, asserts that life (being) is the person's most precious possession; possessing the whole world (having) could not compensate for its loss. If we consider this saying as a continuation of the preceding theme (martyrdom), it would mean that to keep and promote a life of material possessions, with everything they entail, is as nothing in comparison with the loss of the true life. And the ruin of true life consists of infidelity to Jesus and his gospel.

The fact remains that the logion, taken by itself, is not clearly related to the theme of martyrdom. It is better understood as a warning against grasping for gain and against wealth. Luke follows this in his teachings on the subject: a person's life is not made secure by an abundance of material possessions (Luke 12:15; see also the parable of the foolish rich man: Luke 12:16–21). It could be that this is the original *Sitz im Leben*.

d. The fourth declaration (Mark 8:37), the shortest, is the person's exchange (redemption) of his or her life: "And indeed [omitted by Matthew] what can [Matthew:will] a man offer in exchange [redemption] for his soul?"

One can see here an allusion to Psalm 49:8–10: the rich cannot escape death (judgment) even by giving away their entire fortune: "But man could never redeem himself or pay ransom to God: it costs so much to redeem his life, it is beyond him. . . ." In line with the preceding saying, this proverb stresses to an even greater degree the impossibility of guaranteeing true survival by means of riches.

But even if such was its original message, the pericope acquires a slightly different meaning when one considers the particular context in its entirety. The preceding logion stated that one must not ruin one's true life, because winning the entire world could not compensate for such a loss. This logion reaffirms that statement by way of an interrogative exclamation: What possession could suffice for it? To lose one's life (by refusing martyrdom) would be an irreparable catastrophe.

e. The following logion (Mark 8:38, RSV) does not appear in Matthew: "For whoever is ashamed of me and of my words in this adulterous and sinful generation of him will the Son of man also be ashamed, when he comes in the glory of his Father with the holy angels [before the angels of God: Luke 12:9]."

This text brings us back explicitly to the pericope's theme: one must indeed not deny Jesus, not be ashamed of him and his teachings, even when one fears the worst in the face of opposition and persecution. A similar declaration is stated even more clearly in Matthew 10:32–33 and Luke 12:8–9: "So if any one declares himself for me in the presence of men, I will declare myself for him in the presence of my Father in heaven. But the one who disowns me in the presence of men, I will disown in the presence of my Father in heaven" (Matt. 10:32–33).

To be ashamed, to renounce, deny, disown is equivalent concretely to saving one's life, but at the same time losing the most important life—the life of declaring oneself for Jesus. Indeed, such an attitude produces the true loss: the Son of man is in turn ashamed of his disciple; he disowns and does not acknowledge him or her on that most solemn and unique occasion when he comes in his glory.

Matthew, as we have just said, omits this logion; however, he retains the ending (the coming of the Son of man in his glory) with the addition "he will reward each one according to his behavior" (Matt. 16:27). Because of the absence of the first clause ("if anyone is ashamed . . ."), this verse seems to be in a void. The connection with the rest of the section remains unclear.

f. The Synoptics converge (with many variants) in this final declaration (Mark 9:1, RSV), which begins, "Truly, I say to you, . . ." creating a break from the other sayings: "Truly, I say to you, there are some standing here who will not taste death before they see the kingdom of God come with power [Mark; the Son of man coming in his kingdom: Matthew]."

This text does not express a demand, as was generally the case for the preceding logia, but rather, affirms a promise. Those surrounding Jesus (the twelve, the crowd?) will not see death without having witnessed the coming of the kingdom. Is this Jesus' own promise? What is its meaning? Does he mean the Parousia, hoped for by the first Christians? The end of a Judaism centered around the Temple? The inauguration of the kingdom by the resurrection? It is not for us to answer these questions within the framework of a study on radicalism. Let us merely note that in the

Synoptics this verse serves as a direct transition to the Transfiguration narrative.

2. CONCLUSION

The sayings on the conditions of following Jesus are certainly important ones because of their content and the context in which they are placed. To be sure, the six logia are not of the same mold. They have, no doubt, diverse *Sitz im Leben*; the last three, especially, do not easily fit into the general framework. The first three, on the other hand, are close in meaning and give a coherence to the whole. They draw out and transform the others. Whatever their sources and primitive meanings were, these sayings form a unified, composite structure.

As far as the meaning is concerned, one could distinguish at least two levels. From Jesus' mouth, the first two logia no doubt related the absolute demand of preferring him over everything: oneself and one's life, even accepting the most shameful of deaths. Here we touch upon the deepest renunciation asked for the sake of Jesus. According to tradition and the Gospel redactors, the meaning remains the same for the whole collection. (In Luke, the orientation is a moral one: to live as a disciple, even when death is not an imminent threat, is to "take up one's cross daily.") It comes from a perspective of burgeoning persecutions—a perspective attested to especially by the fifth logion.

The third and fourth logia could at their origin have relayed some warnings against riches, but in their final state they share the general meaning: nothing can equal the loss of denying Jesus in order to assert oneself.

The recipients of the message, as we have seen, are the disciples and the crowd—in short, every hearer of Jesus and the gospel. What the meaning originally was eludes us. According to the preachers and the evangelists, however, it is clear: all who want to follow Jesus (by faith assent) must commit themselves to this way.

The unparalleled demand of denying oneself is based on an equally unparalleled reason: "for the sake of Jesus." The pericopes just analyzed are in fact proclamations of the absolute nature of Jesus' relationship to his disciples. Ultimately it can be summarized in two points: Jesus has the right to demand all and the disciples have the duty to accept it. These two points then converge in the promise and the vision of true life found by those who lose their own.

THE DOUBLE TRADITION MATTHEW/LUKE: TO "HATE" ONE'S FATHER AND MOTHER (MATT. 10:37-39)

Another important grouping of radical sayings is peculiar to Matthew/Luke (Matt. 10:37-39). Here other sayings are added to those mentioned above that require self-renunciation (even unto death) represented by these demands: one must "hate" one's next of kin and abandon all of one's possessions.

Some of these sayings are common to both evangelists; others are given only by Luke. Moreover their context is very different. In Matthew the declaration is part of the great missionary discourse (Matt. 10:1-42) and follows the prediction of family persecutions and dissensions. In Luke it is placed in a sort of no-man's land without any details about the circumstances. We can certainly favor Luke's account. He seems to have preserved a Semitic quality closer to the original and he did not insert sayings that possibly circulated alone into a systematic collection.

1. ANALYSIS

In a discourse addressed to the twelve, Matthew connects everything to sayings about Jesus as the cause of dissension (Matt. 10:34-35), sayings that Luke also transmits (Luke 12:51, 53) but without any relationship with the surrounding sayings. Jesus has come "to set a man against his father, a daughter against her mother, a daughter-in-law against her mother-in-law" (Matt. 10:35).

It is no doubt this concept of conflict which evokes the following sayings:

37 He who loves father or mother more than me is not worthy of me; and he who loves son or daughter more than me is not worthy of me;

38 and he who does not take his cross and follow me is not
worthy of me. [RSV]

In Luke, Jesus is on his way to Jerusalem (Luke 14:25) and
turns to the great crowds accompanying him to declare:

26 If anyone comes to me and does not hate his father and
mother, wife and children, and brothers and sisters,
even his own life, he cannot be a disciple of mine.
27 Whoever does not bear his own cross and come after me,
cannot be my disciple. [NEB]

In spite of the different context and presentation, the sayings
are the same. Each of Matthew's three declarations ends with the
sharp phrase: "is not worthy of me." The first two mention
father and mother (v. 37a) and son and daughter (v. 37b). The
third speaks of the taking up of one's cross.

Luke assembles all the family members in one sentence: father,
mother, wife, children, brothers, and sisters. One will notice that
"son or daughter" in Matthew becomes "children" in Luke.
Luke also specifies wife, brothers, and sisters. Moreover, he adds
the expression "his own life" after the list of the next of kin whom
one must hate. On the other hand, his second sentence, with only
a slight variance, is identical to Matthew's third. Luke has only
two declarations here. The third appears in verse 33 of the same
chapter 14.

The literary formation between the two is different. "The one
who loves . . . more than me is not worthy of me" is Matthew's
schema. Luke's form is harsher and directly translated from the
Semitic substrate: "If anyone does not hate . . . he cannot be my
disciple." (John 12:25 presents the same expression: "anyone
who hates his life.")

What takes precedence in these sayings is the demand for severing ties with the next of kin. Matthew and Luke both affirm that
Jesus must be absolutely preferred over the people one holds most
dear. Luke expresses this demand brutally: one cannot come to
Jesus to become his disciple unless one hates those to whom one is
bound by flesh and blood. Luke adds still another mention of the
spouse, brothers, and sisters to Matthew's list. By saying "to love
more than me," Matthew explains (and attenuates) the word

"hate." To hate one's next of kin means to love them less than one loves Jesus, to love them second best.[3]

By adding "even one's own life" to the list, Luke alludes to the triple-tradition verse (losing one's life in order to save it: Mark 8:35) and to what Matthew repeats here in verse 39: "Anyone who finds his life will lose it; anyone who loses his life for my sake will find it."

Quite likely this is the reason Luke omits this saying here only to use it again in another context with a different meaning (Luke 17:33). We have already encountered this saying in the analysis of the second logion of the preceding grouping (pp. 47–48). Matthew's text preserves better the contrast between finding and losing. Matthew 10:39 and 38 as well as Luke 14:27 have already been examined. As a matter of fact, the latter two correspond to the first logion (Mark 3:34) of the grouping analyzed in the preceding pages. They keep the same meaning as previously: to be Jesus' disciple, to "be worthy of him" (Matthew), one must be ready to lose even one's life. This is once again expressed by the image of taking up (Matthew) or carrying (Luke) one's cross—the latter example indicating a time span (Luke 9:23, "daily").

Thus the first part of this small collection introduces a new demand of renunciation: family relationships must recede before Jesus' demands. The second part repeats the already encountered themes (at greater length in Matthew, in a more condensed manner in Luke), themes associated with sayings on family attachments. The two themes seem to be somewhat juxtaposed, unless the cross in this context means renouncing all family attachments for the sake of Jesus.

The Matthew/Luke parallel stops here, for Luke has a longer text. Before giving a third logion on the abandonment of all possessions (Luke 14:33), Luke inserts a double parable (14:28–32). The one who wishes to build a tower must first of all calculate the expense to see if he can bring the construction to completion. Likewise a king marching to war must first of all consider what the possibilities are of winning. These two examples of conventional wisdom are, in this context, an invitation to weigh the enormous cost that the disciple must pay when making a commitment to follow Jesus. These are not meant to dissuade one from the enterprise but to point out how terribly difficult it is and that one must not commit oneself lightly or not be ready to pay, if necessary, with one's life.

Then comes the final logion (the third declaration): "So in the same way, none of you can be my disciple unless he gives up all his possessions."

Constructed like the preceding ones, this logion opens up another area of renunciation. Until now the two evangelists had insisted on the necessary distance to one's family because of the fundamental demand of taking up one's cross. Luke adds (and his is the only Gospel to present this saying) the demand of parting with all one's possessions. The expressions in this logion accentuate the radicality of the demands: "none of you" leaves no room for any exceptions. And one must renounce all one's possessions. As we shall see later, this theme of renunciation is especially emphasized in Luke's Gospel. It is not surprising that it is introduced here and placed next to Jesus' sayings that Luke has in common with Matthew.

Most exegetes believe this absolute saying of the renunciation of all possessions seems to be a Lucan creation interpreting and applying Jesus' desire for detachment from riches to Christians of his time.[4]

2. CONCLUSION

The second grouping (Matthew/Luke) does not lack parallels with the first (Mark 8:34–9:1). In fact the second part (Matt. 10:38–39; Luke 14:26–27, with the adjunct "even his own life") completely reiterates the first two sayings of the Synoptic collection. What is new is the theme of renouncing one's family (Matthew/Luke) and, in Luke alone, the complete renunciation of possessions. The first collection is limited to one theme addressed in various ways: one must lose one's life for the sake of Jesus. The second collection conserves this same theme without dwelling on it, but adds other specific demands applied to two fundamental dimensions of human existence: interpersonal bonds and possessions.

What do we understand these demands to mean? We shall not return to the already covered theme of the cross and losing one's life. But what renunciation of family and possessions is required? In Matthew the context throws some light on the question (Matt. 10:34–36): Jesus' coming introduces division in the midst of families; he sets members against each other. In such heartrending situations the disciple's choice is clearly indicated. In order to be worthy of the Master, one must choose him and love him more than those nearest and most dear. Luke's version places these sayings of Jesus to the crowds outside of any context that could clarify them. They also are more absolute and blunt. The more complete list of those whom one must leave behind, the word "hate" (as in John 12:25, it is the only case in the Gospels where the disciple is ordered to "hate"), and the last logion, "renounce all one's possessions" (Luke 14:33), strongly emphasize the severing of ties that must take place if one wants to be a disciple in these very delicate situations. In short, Matthew indicates situations where these ruptures occur; Luke seems to require them as absolutes.

Even more evident is that the recipients in each account are not quite the same. For Matthew they are the twelve, even though the discourse is addressed concretely to the missionary Christians and, beyond them, to all believers who encounter family dissensions. Luke, according to his custom, generalizes. Everything takes place on the way to Jerusalem (13:22). While great crowds accompany him (14:25) Jesus turns and speaks to them. It is to the crowds that these demands are obviously intended. Let us note once again that these narratives are meant to challenge not only the original recipients, but beyond them, all those who read these sayings.

EUNUCHS FOR THE SAKE OF THE KINGDOM (MATT. 19:10–12)

Immediately before the third Passion prediction is a coherent and continuous series of teachings present in all the Synoptics (Mark 10:2–31) concerning divorce (Luke omits this pericope), children, the call to sell everything, the danger of riches, the reward promised for renunciation. There is a logical pattern of thought here to which Jesus' teachings on family (pericopes on marriage, divorce, children) and possessions (the other pericopes) are aligned. One will notice that both themes are assembled in Luke (14:25-33) in the text examined in the preceding pages.

After Jesus' declarations on marriage and divorce (Mark 10:2-13), Matthew alone inserts the strange saying on eunuchs (Matt. 19:10-12). The disciples, disturbed by the demands on marriage, which allow for neither repudiation (divorce) nor remarriage, object: "If that is how things are between husband and wife, it is not advisable to marry" (v. 10). Jesus replies:

11 It is not everyone who can accept what I have said, but only those to whom it is granted.

12 There are eunuchs born that way from their mother's womb, there are eunuchs made so by men and there are eunuchs who have made themselves that way for the sake of the kingdom of heaven. Let anyone accept this who can.

What does this saying mean? According to the common exegetical interpretation, it acknowledges and approves the fact of not marrying on account of (or for the sake of) the kingdom of heaven.[5] This interpretation is articulated as follows. After the declaration on monogamous marriage according to God's original plan (Matt. 19:4-6) and in response to the Pharisees' objection, citing the divorce authorized by Moses (v. 7), Jesus gives a legalistic rule of conduct that excludes divorce and remarriage, except in the case of "fornication" (*porneia*, v. 9). Then comes a teaching that extends and completes the doctrine on the demands of marriage. There is still another option for the disciples: not to marry for the sake of the kingdom of heaven.

To the disillusionment of the disciples, who remark that "it is advisable not to marry" (v. 10), since divorce and remarriage are excluded, Jesus replies that not everyone can grasp what they are saying, for it is deeper than they think. Only those to whom it is given by God understand it. There are indeed eunuchs by birth (and this in the physical meaning of the word); others are so because they were castrated. There is still a third category: those who make themselves eunuchs (this time in the figurative meaning of not marrying) because of the kingdom. The text ends by an invitation, quite in the Matthean style, to make an effort to receive and understand this spiritually. "Let anyone accept this who can."[6]

The central portion of the declaration (the triple saying on eunuchs) is by itself simply an observation. Apart from the two known categories of eunuchs, there are some persons who, because of religious motivations (the kingdom), seem to be unsuited to marriage. It is, then, essentially for reason of a spiritual incapacity. The statements "It is not everyone who can accept what I have said" (v. 10), and "Let anyone accept this who can" (v. 12) are at once an invitation and an observation. The understanding and the exercise of this logion pertain to only a few, those to whom it is given by God. For the first time—and this will be the only case in the Gospels—we encounter Jesus proposing a situation, an attitude, as a possible option that, and this is said explicitly, is not required of everyone. At any rate, this logion adds a new dimension to the already drastic sayings about family: to live without getting married for the sake of the kingdom.

This motivation "for the sake of the kingdom" requires some explanation. In the Synoptic Gospels, the kingdom of God is the new salvific situation inaugurated by Jesus' coming and preaching. The decision to live as a eunuch (not to marry) is connected to this new situation, to the kingdom. Could one translate "on account of the kingdom" as "because the reality of it opens new perspectives and offers new possibilities"? Or else "for the sake of the kingdom" as "in order fully to participate in it or serve it better"? The Greek particle *dia* allows for the two meanings, but the first seems to fit the context better. It is the presence of the kingdom that explains the fact of remaining unmarried and its possibility.

Given the image's forceful character, the declaration's Semitic structure (a type of numerical proverb), as well as the teaching's strangeness and novelty, one might think that the essence of this saying finds its source in Jesus himself and is not a creation of the community.

What remains now is to situate this saying in its original context if possible. Unless one considers it as a prophecy of Christian celibacy (which was in fact being practiced from the very beginning of Christianity), one must suppose that it finds its roots in the life and teachings of Jesus.

Since Jesus was not married, it would be surprising if such nonconformity were not maliciously singled out by his adversaries. Was he not accused of being a "glutton and a drunkard" (Matt. 11:19)? Hence, he could have also been scornfully called a eunuch. Jesus may have turned the word into a kind of proverb, retorting that there were eunuchs by birth, others who were castrated, and some who lived in this way because of the kingdom. Not everyone, to be sure, can understand such behavior! Thus initially the logion could have been a self-defense, a positive judgment on Jesus' celibacy revealing his motivation: the experience of the kingdom of heaven.[7]

This saying of Jesus was preserved and applied, outside its original context, to the celibates of the first Christian communities in a setting that emphasized the gratuitous and nonobligatory dimension of celibacy.

Whatever these hypotheses imply, it is important to note that Matthew presents in Jesus' teachings a radicalism whose forceful and difficult character is confirmed by the image utilized. Let us add that even though it is Matthew who mentions eunuchs, some of Luke's emphases are in the same vein. Thus, when in a Synoptic collection (Mark 10:29), Mark/Matthew speak of leaving house, brother, sister, father, mother, children, and fields, Luke adds the word "wife" to the list (Luke 18:29). Likewise, for the text already commented upon, which he holds in common with Matthew, Luke adds "wife" to the list of those whom one must "hate" (Luke 14:26). And again, in the passage on marriage and resurrection ("for when they rise from the dead, men and women do not marry," Mark 12:25), Luke introduces an emphatic opposition between "the children of this world [who] take wives and husbands" and "those who are judged worthy of a place in the other world and in the resurrection from the dead [who] do not marry" (Luke 20:34–35). Some see in this formula a direct invitation to celibacy because, for Luke, "abstention from marriage is not only for those who have risen from the dead but also those who are judged worthy to participate in the future world in this life."[8]

Let us conclude this summary analysis with two observations.

The fact of becoming a eunuch because of the kingdom seems to be a radical renunciation, but one that is possible and commendable. It is expressly portrayed as a gift granted not to everyone "but only those to whom it is given" (Matt. 19:11). It is the only passage in the Gospel where one meets such a distinction.

GENERAL CONCLUSION

The renunciations studied in this chapter are concentrated in three areas. The disciple must first of all renounce self, his or her own life: such is the message of the first collection (in the triple tradition: Mark 8:34–9:1). As an extension of this absolute renunciation comes the sacrifice of one's closest natural relationships (in the double tradition: Matt. 10: 37–39) and even the decision not to marry (Matt. 19:10–12). To this Luke adds the necessity of abandoning all one's possessions (Luke 14:33).

Despite slight differences in each of the Gospels about who the recipients are (for Matthew they are always the disciples, the twelve: 16:24; 10:1; 19:10; for Mark, the disciples and the crowd: 8:34; for Luke, everyone: 9:23, or the crowd: 14:25), ultimately the demands are addressed to the hearers and readers of the Gospel.

It is always the relationship with the person of Jesus that serves as the basis for such demands: to be his disciple, to follow in his footsteps, to be worthy of him. It is for the sake of the kingdom that one goes so far. The renunciations, the breaking of ties, the abandonments required have meaning only in this perspective. Nowhere are rewards mentioned; the only promise that surfaces is the paradoxical "whoever loses himself will find himself." We are indeed confronted with total radicalism resting on unconditional adherence to a person. The one who makes these demands implicitly presents himself as the root and center. What person would dare to do so?

NOTES

1. In Greek *elthein*, "to come," is a conclusive action in Mark/Matthew; *erchesthai*, "to walk," is a lasting action in Luke.

2. This position by Bultmann and numerous other exegetes (Taylor, Schlatter, Manson, Schulz) seems the most solid one to us. According to E. Dinkler's hypothesis in "Jesus Wort vom Kreuztragen," *Neutestamentliche Studien für Rudolf Bultmann* (Berlin: BZNW 21, 1954), pp. 110-29, it would be a mark or tattoo in the shape of a cross (or tau) signifying that one belongs to Jesus. This hypothesis is too farfetched to be convincing. But Dinkler's study remains a basic one for analysis of the givens and various opinions.

3. In the context, this is the meaning of the Semitic expression "to hate." See A. Schulz, *Nachfolgen und Nachame* (Munich: Kösel, 1962), p. 80.

4. A detailed account of the exegetical question can be found in J. Dupont, "Renoncer à tous ses biens," *Nouvelle Revue Théologique* 93 (1971): 586-670.

5. For a general study on celibacy, see T. Matura, "Le célibat dans le Nouveau Testament d'après l'exégèse récente," *Nouvelle Revue Théologique* 97 (1975): 481-500, 593-604. The study on Matt. 19:10-12 can be found on pp. 487-96.

6. Parallels in Matt. 11:14-15; 13:19, 43; 24:15.

7. J. Blinzler's hypothesis is analyzed in Matura, "Le célibat," pp. 489-50.

8. Boismard, *Synopse de quatre évangiles en français*, 2 vols. (Paris: Cerf, 1972), 2:349.

5

Attitudes toward Material Possessions

The simple enumeration (pp. 21–22) of the Synoptic teachings on wealth and poverty, if only by their quantity, has already given us a sense of their importance. In this chapter we shall examine the various instructions on this theme that are retained by the double and triple tradition and, finally, the texts peculiar to Luke.

THE SYNOPTIC COLLECTION

While analyzing the pericope on eunuchs (Matt. 19:10–12; see pp. 56–60), we noticed a series of various teachings on marriage, children, the call to sell everything, the danger of riches, the reward promised for detachment (Mark 10:2–31). As we can see, these passages, including the one on the indissolubility of marriage, form a collection of the radical demands of Jesus. The pericopes on children and eunuchs have already been examined; the ones on divorce will be examined later. We shall now concentrate on the group concerning the use of possessions (Mark 10:17–31). This collection is composed of three different but closely connected narratives: the call of the rich man (Mark 10:17–22); the danger of riches (Mark 10:23–27); the reward promised for detachment (Mark 10:28–31).

1. THE CALL OF THE RICH MAN (MARK 10:17–22)[1]

This episode is narrated in an almost identical way by Mark/Luke; Matthew's presentation is unique.

Mark/Luke

The concrete situation is vague in the three Gospels. Someone (Mark/Matthew), a member of the ruling class (mentioned as being rich, Luke 18:23) approaches Jesus with a question: "Good Teacher, what shall I do to inherit eternal life?" (RSV). One will notice that this concern to obtain eternal life does not appear elsewhere apart from this text.

Jesus' answer can be divided into two parts. In the first, which seems a digression (Mark 10:18), Jesus reacts to the title given to him: "Why do you call me good? No one is good but God alone." Jesus distinguishes himself from and subordinates himself to God: only God can be called "good" in the fullest sense of the word. Certainly we have here one of Jesus' authentic sayings, for it is difficult to imagine the Christian community inventing a declaration that would seem to diminish Jesus. This is one of those "humble" sayings where Jesus presents himself as different from and inferior to God (see also the saying on his ignorance about the day of judgment: Mark 13:32; Matt. 24:36, but not in Luke).

The second part directly responds to the question, What must one do? "You know the commandments of the Torah: they must be observed." Six commandments are then enumerated: do not kill, do not commit adultery, do not steal, do not bear false witness, do not defraud (omitted by Luke), and honor father and mother (Mark 10:19).

The dialogue resumes with the man's affirmation (Mark 10:20): "All these I have observed from my youth" (RSV). Pursuing his answer to the initial question, Jesus declares that to obtain eternal life, observance of the commandments is not sufficient: "You lack one thing; go, sell what you have ["all you have," Luke] and give ["distribute," Luke] to the poor, and you will have treasure in heaven; and come, follow me" (RSV).

Jesus' demand comprises three connecting steps: sell one's possessions; distribute them to the poor; become a disciple. There is, likewise, the promise of reward (treasure), an idea we encounter later (Matt. 6:19–21). Selling one's goods is not motivated out of scorn for possessions but is done for the purpose of sharing, to give, distribute the fruit of it to the poor. This is the condition for becoming Jesus' disciple and following him. Is this a call addressed to a real person (whose name was not preserved) to become part of the special group of disciples? Or are we faced with a behavioral model proposed to all believers? We shall have to return later to this question. For the moment, let us unhesitatingly assert that since these demands (selling all, giving it to the poor, becoming a disciple) are necessary to obtain eternal life, they are obviously intended for all hearers of the gospel.

At any rate, the man does not accept Jesus' conditions: "But his face fell at these words and he went away sad, for he was a man of great wealth." The fact of having many possessions ("he was very rich," Luke) prevented the man from being a disciple and ultimately obtaining eternal life. This last verse already prepares for the pericope that follows on the danger of riches.

Matthew (Matt. 19:16–22)

Matthew's presentation is more complex compared with the relatively simple narrative above. The evangelist wants to avoid Jesus' embarrassing declaration that only God is good and present a teaching on the two steps of abandoning riches.

In effect the man's question is a different one (v. 16): "Teacher, what good deed must I do, to have eternal life?" (RSV). Jesus is not the one called good, but rather, he is questioned on what is good. Thus his first answer is, "Why do you ask me about what is good? There is one alone who is good" (v. 17). This last sentence is not really related to what preceded but is a vestige of the primitive text as Mark/Luke report it.

Jesus' answer to the question "What good deed must I do to have eternal life?" is divided into two parts. The first part is "If you wish to enter into life, keep the commandments." To enter into life, it is indispensable to keep the commandments. "Which [commandments]?" the man asks. Jesus replies, quoting the same preceding list. This time, however, he adds the commandment that summarizes the entire Law, "You must love your neighbor as yourself," a commandment that, in principle, assumes almsgiving and sharing with others who are poorer. The "young man" (Matthew perhaps is transforming the expression "since my youth" used by Mark/Luke) answers, "All these I have observed; what do I still lack?"

Thus we have the introduction for the second part of the

answer. Jesus declares (Matt. 19:21): "If you wish to be perfect, go and sell what you own and give the money to the poor, and you will have treasure in heaven; then come, follow me." Although the passage is identical to the demand in Mark/Luke, the initial clause, peculiar to Matthew, is to be noted: "If you wish to be perfect, . . ." All three evangelists end with the sadness of the "young man" (Matt. 19:22).

Apart from the modifications to the beginning (the question on what is good), the major change in Matthew is the distinction made between the conditions required "to have life" and those required "to be perfect." For Mark/Luke, both the observance of the commandments and the selling of one's possessions are required to "inherit eternal life." What does this imply?

In the first part of the response (Matt. 19:18-19), the observance of the Law is required. Adding the commandment of love, which sums up the Law and the prophets (only Matt. 22:40), seems strange unless its precise intent is to prepare for what follows—namely, that true love of neighbor requires selling and sharing one's possessions.

The second part (Matt. 19:21) indicates what the inquirer lacks to be "perfect." We encounter the word "perfect" (*teleios*) only twice in the Synoptic Gospels, both times in Matthew: in the encounter with the rich young man and in the Sermon on the Mount (Matt. 5:48), where it is said, "You must therefore be perfect just as your heavenly Father is perfect." This text concludes six antitheses (Matt. 45:20-47)—of which we shall speak later—that put the demands of the Mosaic Law in opposition to the far more radical demands required of Jesus' disciples. In this context, to be perfect means to fulfill the new justice, the one greater than that of the scribes and the Pharisees. Fulfilling this justice is necessary in order to enter the kingdom of heaven (Matt. 5:20). Thus, to be perfect—meaning to become Jesus' disciple and try to do what he asks—is necessary for salvation. It is difficult to imagine that the meaning of the word "perfect" is a different one in the second text (Matt. 19:21). When Jesus says to the young man that in order to be perfect one must be rid of one's possessions, share with the poor, and begin to follow his leading, he is not indicating a path reserved for an exclusive class of people. He is not propos-

ing a supererogatory or optional behavior. As in the Sermon on
the Mount, Jesus affirms that, while observance of the Law may
have been necessary, it is not sufficient. To be perfect—that is, to
become Jesus' disciple (in the sense of a believing Christian)—one
must necessarily abandon and share one's possessions.

Such is, at least, the exegetical explanation that seems to us the
most solid. Otherwise we would have to give the word "perfect" a
meaning that it does not have in the Gospels and assume that
Matthew totally modified the Mark/Luke presentation (which
does not distinguish two categories of that which is required to
have life and that which is necessary to be perfect).[2]

Conclusion

These few exegetical conclusions, which will be clarified again
later (especially after the analysis of the two following pericopes),
give us the opportunity to emphasize certain already established
points.

The focal point to which the entire narrative leads is verse 21:
"Go, and sell what you own and give the money to the poor, and
you will have treasure in heaven; then come, follow me." The
narrative, with the differences that we have noted, is organized
around and a function of this declaration. To enter into life, to be
part of the new existence which Jesus proposes (to be perfect), one
must completely abandon all one's possessions. This divestiture is
not arbitrary. It must be done in relation to those who are in want,
the poor. It is, therefore, less a question of renunciation or divestiture than of a gift. One sells one's belongings in order to give
them away. A true treasure is reserved in the world to come for
those who do so, and even now they join the group of disciples.

Such a demand surely seems absolute. The triple tradition
presents it here in a narrative that, strictly speaking, could rele-
gate it to only one particular concrete situation. But in Luke one
finds the same declaration repeated twice—as a categorical statement and as a general application:

Sell your possessions and give alms.
Get yourselves purses that do not wear out,
   treasure that will not fail you, in heaven . . . [Luke 12:33].

So in the same way, none of you can be my disciple
unless he gives up all his possessions [Luke 14:33].

The resemblance of these two sayings with Matthew 19:21 is
striking. The first, *"Sell* your possessions . . . *give* alms . . .
treasure . . . in heaven," repeats almost word for word verse 21:
". . . *sell* what you own and *give* the money to the poor, and you
will have *treasure* in heaven." The second specifies that this renunciation is part of becoming a disciple—in the wider sense; that
is, to be a Christian—(see discussion on pp. 55–56), which sheds
light on the final clause of the declaration in Matthew 19:21:
"come, follow me." As one can see, Jesus' demand (as exorbitant
as it may seem), illustrated by the pericope of the rich man, seems
to have been part of his teaching intended for everyone.

It is true that current interpretation sees in this narrative two
complementary ways: to enter into life (salvation), it is necessary
to observe the commandments; to be "perfect" (do more and
better), one must abandon one's possessions and become Jesus'
disciple. Examination of the text shows us the weakness of such
an exegesis. The Mark/Luke narrative does not make this distinction whatsoever. Jesus' two-part response converges into a single
question: What must one do to obtain life? In Matthew, without
doubt, there does seem to be a twofold response: there is an ordinary way and a perfect way. We, however, tend to think that,
along the lines of the Sermon on the Mount, observance of the
Law (necessary but insufficient) and the perfection entailed in
becoming Jesus' disciple (completely disposed to share everything
with the poor) go together. At the same time that he affirms the
Law for his Judeo-Christian readers, Matthew clearly indicates
the necessity of going beyond it by distributing one's possessions
to the poor and in becoming Jesus' disciple.

The question of the historical kernel of the narrative remains to
be answered. Are we encountering the traces of some true-life
situation or is this a discipleship teaching presented in the form of
an ideal "scene," a "paradigm" (as in Matt. 8:22; see p. 30)? The
answer to this question naturally influences the very meaning of
the teaching. If there is a real-life situation behind the episode, it
is an individual instance that does not necessarily apply to other

situations. If, on the other hand, we are faced with a teaching illustrated by an example, then general application seems warranted. Insofar as these unsolvable questions are concerned, let us assume (and what follows will confirm this) that the narrative stands as an example.

2. THE DANGER OF RICHES (MARK 10:23–27)[3]

The pericope on the rich man is immediately followed by a teaching that riches are an obstacle to entering the kingdom. Using Mark's text as a basis, we shall briefly analyze this teaching.

The narrative is linked with what precedes it: the disappointed man goes away (v. 22). In Luke (18:24), where he does not go away, Jesus looks at him and makes this reflection: "How hard it is for those who have riches to enter the kingdom of God!" (RSV). If it were necessary, this reflection would show that for the evangelists (even for Matthew), the rich man, by his refusal, risks not only losing the way of perfection but also eternal life.

Mark's subsequent verse (without parallels in Matthew/Luke) describes the disciples astonishment at these words. Mark offers a new thought of Jesus, repeating almost word for word but generalizing the saying of Luke 18:23: "My children, how hard it is to enter the kingdom of God!" (Mark 10:24). In an absolute sense this affirmation relates the general difficulty of attaining salvation (parallel in Luke 13:23–24).

The three traditions converge in Luke 13:24: "It is easier for a camel to pass through the eye of a needle than for a rich man to enter the kingdom of God." This paradoxical declaration expresses through hyperbole essentially the same idea as verse 23, the difficulty for the rich to attain salvation.

The disciples react strongly (the second time in Mark, the first in Matthew/Luke): "they were more astonished than ever" (Mark/Matthew; Luke does not mention this astonishment). They then say, "In that case . . . who can be saved?" This astonishment is indeed strange. The surprise, as it is expressed in the text, should apply to the general difficulty of being saved. If it were merely the difficulty stemming from wealth, the surprise would be irrelevant, for riches did not abound in the Christian community and the Jewish world in general at that time. One has the impression of encountering two different sayings, one concerning the general difficulty of being saved, the other concerning the particular difficulties of wealth.

The pericope concludes with a new declaration by Jesus (v. 27): "For men," he said "it is impossible, but not for God: because everything is possible for God. "

The narrative, as we have noticed, is a composite one. Quite likely there is a more or less successful fusion (especially in Mark) of two connected but distinct declarations. The first declares wealth as an obstacle to salvation: it is difficult for a rich man to enter the kingdom (v. 23) . . . more difficult than for a camel to pass through the eye of a needle (v. 25). The second, more absolute, affirms the general difficulty of being saved (v. 24). The stupefaction expressed (vv. 24, 26) is normally associated with the latter.

In spite of these two lines of thought, the meaning is clear. In its existing state, the text after the episode of the rich man reaffirms the opposition between the state of discipleship (his entry into the kingdom) and wealth. The extraordinary image of the camel and the needle (for a Palestinian, the largest animal and the smallest hole), the unqualified, absolute declaration, and the difficulty of applying and interpreting it clearly demonstrate that the saying was not created by a community but was transmitted as if coming from the Lord. We will see later how Luke and, to a lesser degree, Matthew orchestrate this type of Jesus' teaching on wealth. Texts of this type are not prevalent in the Synoptic tradition, but the mere fact that a collection of such demanding teachings does exist is significant.

Let us also note that the teaching of this pericope, with its link to the preceding one, pushes us to interpret the latter as a necessary model for all disciples. To enter into the kingdom one must surrender one's possessions and share them with the poor.

3. THE REWARD PROMISED FOR DETACHMENT (MARK 10:28-31)

In contrast with the rich man who refused to sell his possessions, and after describing how the wealthy risk losing salvation, the Synoptic tradition presents the reward promised to those who have left everything for the sake of Jesus.

Even if at first glance the narrative appears simple, soon we again encounter many complexities. The link with the preceding pericope is sure: faced with Jesus' declaration on the difficulty of salvation for the rich, Peter begins by saying, "We have left everything and followed you." (Matthew adds, "What are we to have, then?") The three Synoptics, with numerous variants, show Jesus seemingly addressing neither Peter nor the twelve but "everyone." In Mark the text reads as follows (vv. 29–30):

29 Truly, I say to you, there is no one who has left house or brothers or sisters or mother or father or children or lands for my sake and for the gospel,

30 who will not receive a hundredfold now in this time, houses and brothers and sisters and mothers and children and lands, with persecutions, and in the age to come eternal life. [RSV]

Luke's version (18:29–30) is quite close to Mark's except that the list is not repeated:

29 I tell you solemnly, there is no one who has left house, wife, brothers, parents or children for the sake of the kingdom of God

30 who will not be given repayment many times over in this present time and, in the world to come, eternal life.

In Matthew (19:28–29), on the other hand, the variants are important:

28 I tell you this . . . anyone

29 who has left brothers or sisters, father, mother or children, land or houses for the sake of my name will be repaid many times over, and gain eternal life. [NEB]

On the whole, the list of persons and things to be sacrificed is identical, although Luke omits the fields, rearranges the family members, and adds "wife." The motivation for leaving everything remains the same even if it is expressed differently: for my sake, for the sake of my name, the gospel (see also Mark 8:35), the kingdom.

The differences are accentuated by the "many times" of Matthew/Luke, which becomes "a hundredfold" in Mark. But the most important difference is the distinction of a double reward in Mark/Luke. For Matthew, the one who has left everything will simply receive "many times over" and "eternal life." "Many times over" and "life" seem repetitious, synonymous. Mark/Luke, however, express two distinct situations. In this time (Mark adds emphasis with "now"), what one has left will be given back "many times over" (or "a hundredfold" in Mark). "In this time" would obviously designate the present life as opposed to the "age to come." Mark then adds the somewhat ironic clause "with persecutions," which, though in a different way, is part of rediscovering the family and material possessions left behind. The promises of "eternal life" apply to the world to come. (This expression is very Johannine; eternal life is encountered in the Synoptics only in Mark 10:17,30. See also Matt. 25:46; Luke 10:25.)

We have omitted most of verse 28 in Matthew's text—the only Gospel with this insert between Peter's request and the general promise of a reward. In the verse explicitly addressed to the twelve, Jesus says: "Truly, I say to you, in the new world, when the Son of man shall sit on his glorious throne, you who have followed me will also sit on twelve thrones, judging the twelve tribes of Israel" (RSV).

Thus in Matthew two different logia are juxtaposed. The first attributes the roles of eschatological judges of Israel to the twelve who have followed Jesus (v. 28). The second promises a reward to those who have left everything (v. 29). The logion on the eschatological role of the apostles is likewise given by Luke, though accompanied by other promises and in a different context (the Last Supper, after the declaration on the great who must serve: Luke 22:24–30; see p. 37).

Returning to the text as a whole, we notice that the narrative serves as a framework for the focal sentence, the promise. But this promise is preceded by a preliminary condition essential to our purpose. The promise is offered to whoever will renounce their family and material possessions for the sake of Jesus and the kingdom he inaugurates. In the previously analyzed passage (Matt. 10:37–39), one needed to hate (or love less) the members of one's family (see pp. 52–56). To this demand Luke adds leaving all one's possessions (Luke 14:33). Here the meaning of this demand is specified: there are in fact some who actually leave their family. A list follows, which hammers the point: brothers, sisters, mother, father, children (in Matthew, an order of increasing proximity?). Luke has a different order: wife, brother, parents, children. The material possessions left behind include house ("houses" in Matthew) and land.

The text then assumes a situation: there are indeed those who, for the sake of the kingdom, have severed family ties—even those of marriage—and have left their possessions behind. The theme of "coming after Jesus," "following him," is not explicitly mentioned, but this breaking of ties has taken place because of him.

The promise is addressed to these and to all those who do likewise. In Matthew it is simple, for what they have abandoned is nothing compared to what they are promised: eternal life. The idea of a reward from God reserved for those who accomplish good works (prayer, fasting, almsgiving), can be found elsewhere in Matthew's Gospel (Matt. 6:1, 4, 6, 18). The nature of this reward is not specified other than eternal life with God—a topic about which the Synoptic writers remain very discreet.

Apart from eternal life, promised for "the world to come," Mark and Luke propose a reward for the present life. What does it mean to receive "many times over" (Luke) or "a hundredfold" (Mark) "houses and brothers and sisters and mothers and children and lands, with persecutions" (Mark 10:30)? Unless one falls into gross literalism, it is clear that it can only be that a new type of family (Christian community) opens up to the one who has left family according to the flesh. It is with this meaning in mind that the saying concerning Jesus himself must be understood: "Who are my mother and my brothers? . . . Anyone who does the will of God, that person is my brother and sister and mother" (Mark 3:33, 35).

A parallel line of thinking (the conviction that the one who leaves, who is divested of everything to proclaim the coming of the kingdom is assured material welfare) has already been mentioned in the missionary discourse: "the laborer deserves his food" (Matt. 10:10); "stay in the same house, taking what food and drink they have to offer" (Luke 10:7; see p. 32). Thus the idea of reward understood as a new fraternal community, a certainty that the necessities will not be lacking, is not foreign to either the gospel tradition or Jesus' own teaching.

The form that this logion takes in Mark owes a great deal to the experience of the community. Those who, for Jesus and for the sake of the kingdom, have left (often painfully) their family and their possessions, do not remain alone; even in the midst of persecutions, they find an immense community of Christian brothers and sisters. Because of this, they lack nothing.

4. OVERVIEW OF THE THREE PERICOPES

Having covered the three texts, one is initially struck by the unity of theme. Not that this is immediately manifest. On the contrary, we have seen that each text coalesced from at least two logia of different origins. But by means of redactional rearranging and transforming, the collection forms a coherent whole focused on the problem of wealth: how one utilizes it; how one gives it up. The Synoptic tradition wanted to reassemble Jesus' instructions on this theme.

The demands presented in this series involve, first, material possessions and, second, the family. Jesus' disciples, so as not to lose the new life and perfection, must divest themselves of all their possessions in order to share them with the poor. The rich man failed to do this. However, the twelve and others did so, and a reward is promised to them. At any rate, wealth is an obstacle to salvation that only God can overcome. The radicalism of such subject matter is obvious and nothing in the text tempers it. As for the family, we see that the demands of Matthew 10:37 (anyone who loves father or mother more than Jesus) were understood and practiced literally in the community. The severing of ties implied for the twelve (Mark 1:20) was concretely lived, since there were some who had left "wife, brothers, parents or children" (Luke 18:29).

The problem of the recipients is a difficult one. We have already touched upon it in the narrative of the rich man. Though initially it seems to be a "lost vocation," is it not, rather, an illustration (as in the three cases of Luke 9:57–62) of the conditions necessary for discipleship?

In its existing state and context (the two other pericopes), the passage seems to present demands that apply to whomever is committed to following Jesus. The subsequent instructions (danger of riches, promised reward), though addressed to the twelve, have an undeniably universal bearing: it is difficult for any rich person to enter the kingdom; everyone who renounces family and material possessions will have eternal life.

As we can see, we have encountered a core of teachings that no Christians will ever be able to integrate fully into their experience.

There are two types of motivation upon which these gestures (of breaking human and economic ties) are based. The first, encountered almost everywhere, is Jesus, the kingdom, and the gospel. The second, peculiar to this collection, is new and rare in the Gospels. The rich are asked to sell their possessions, distribute them to the poor, and follow Jesus in order to have eternal life (Mark/Luke) and to be perfect (Matthew), that is, to live according to a new justice. This is how they will have a treasure in heaven (reward). Likewise, the rich should divest themselves of their wealth, for otherwise it will be difficult for them to enter God's kingdom. Thus what emerges here is an ethical concern: What must one do (and what is best) that will lead one into discipleship (perfection) and true life?

5. THE SEDUCTION OF WEALTH

Before examining the double tradition, we must also mention the Synoptic reference to wealth as a "seduction" or a "deception" (*apatè*, a rather frequent word in the Pauline epistles: Eph. 4:22; Col. 2:8; 2 Thess. 2:10; Heb. 3:13). It is found in the explanation of the parable of the sower (Mark 4:13–20). The seed fallen in the midst of thorns is choked by them and rendered unproductive. These thorns are identified by Mark as "the worries of this world, the lure of riches and all the other passions" (Mark 4:19). Although Matthew (13:22) omits the mention of unruly passions, he is in agreement with the rest of Mark's text. Luke speaks of the "worries, riches, and pleasures of life" (Luke 8:14).

This moral commentary of the parable of the sower depicts three categories of hearers of the gospel in the primitive community: those who refuse to hear the message (Mark 4:15); those who cannot stand firm during persecution (Mark 4:19); and finally, those who let themselves be taken by the worries of life (Mark

4:19). Among these worries wealth has a place of its own, for it not only preoccupies but, even more, seduces. Luke, who omits the word "seduction," is direct in saying that riches choke the Word.

This clause gives us an idea of what the primitive community was thinking on the subject of the wealth of its members: it emerges as a major obstacle, if not to the reception at least to the growth and fruitfulness of the message. Riches seduce the heart, choke and sterilize the Word. One can never be cautious enough with them.

THE DOUBLE TRADITION: MATTHEW/LUKE

A certain number of teachings on wealth and poverty have been transmitted by Matthew/Luke. This is the case in the Beatitude of the poor and other teachings that Matthew places in the Sermon on the Mount (Matt. 5:3; 6:19–34)—teachings that Luke distributes in three different contexts (Luke 11:34–36; 12:22–34; 16:13). For the sake of convenience we shall follow Matthew's order while indicating, of course, the Lucan peculiarities.

1. HAPPY ARE THE POOR—WOE TO THE RICH (MATT. 5:3)[4]

One occasionally hears of the "radicalism of the Beatitudes." We shall hold off on this subject, returning to it when we treat the Beatitudes as a whole (see chap. 6). Here we shall broach only those touching on the theme of poverty. Matthew has nine Beatitudes (Matt. 5:3–12); Luke proposes four, with four curses as antitheses (Luke 6:20–26). There is a general agreement among exegetes on the fact that Luke stays closer to what Jesus initially proclaimed. He presents three "blessings": the poor, the hungry, the afflicted are proclaimed as the beneficiaries of the good news brought by Jesus. The radical changes that he inaugurates are their concern. In the synagogue of Nazareth, according to Luke's statement (Luke 4:16–21), and responding to those sent by John the Baptist (Matt. 11:2–5), Jesus proclaims himself as the messenger of whom Isaiah spoke (Isa. 61:1–2; cf. Isa. 57:15), entrusted to "bring good news to the poor . . . to bind up hearts that are broken . . . to comfort all those who mourn."

The Beatitudes return to this theme in the form of felicitations or congratulations. The happiness, the felicity of the kingdom is intended for those who are in misfortune, in poverty, hunger, tears. To these proclamations that Jesus could have pronounced in such circumstances, aware that by his person and his mission he was inaugurating a new age, another blessing was added—a blessing of the persecuted—addressed to the situation of the first disciples. Luke probably completed the presentation of the Beatitudes with the contrasting prediction of the calamities awaiting the self-satisfied and rapacious rich. Luke, moreover, directed the Beatitudes—initially for all people in need—especially toward the disciples (Jesus addresses them in the second person "fixing his eyes on his disciples," Luke 6:20), meaning toward the Christians of his time, who in fact found themselves in such situations.

Matthew introduces four other Beatitudes (the meek, the merciful, the pure in heart, the peacemakers) and repeats the one for the persecuted, conferring quite a different meaning on them. Luke refers to material situations or conditions in which persons (disciples) find themselves (poverty, hunger, affliction, persecution) and where God's intervention in Jesus can liberate them and provide happiness. Matthew refers to dispositions required of the disciple for entry into the kingdom.

This far too brief presentation of the critico-literary problems of the Beatitudes is indispensable to situate our present concern— namely, poverty in the Beatitudes. If, according to our initial criteria, we speak of radicalism only when it is a disposition or an attitude that someone has acquired, one must then conclude that in Luke's presentation poverty (material), hunger, tears, and persecution are not voluntary qualities or decisions but unjust situations that God will remedy by reason of his justice and by means of Jesus' mission.

In contrast, the condition of the rich emerges as the unhappy one: they have found their happiness and expect nothing more. Such an observation is indirectly an imperative invitation to change one's situation, particularly by abandoning one's self-sufficiency and riches, in order to receive salvation.

Matthew functions differently. For him, poverty in spirit, like meekness and humility (the three are almost synonymous), is a disposition of the heart that the disciple must acquire to enjoy true happiness now, and be worthy to receive the future promises God has made.

Thus the Beatitude of poverty in Luke is indicative neither of a radical demand nor of a mode of conduct. It is a proclamation of happiness for people (and in fact independent of them) who find themselves in a state of want or need, for God is ready to fulfill their desires. If there is a radicalism, one should, rather, look for it in Matthew; although for him it is less material poverty than the humility, resignation, and patience of "the one who bows his head, submits humbly rather than becoming stiff-necked and resistant."[5]

2. ADVICE TO THE RICH AND THE POOR (MATT. 6:19-34)

In the Sermon on the Mount, Matthew assembles four pericopes, which all directly or indirectly relate to the question of riches: the true treasure (Matt. 6:19-21); the eye as lamp of the body (Matt. 6:22-23); God and money (Matt. 6:24); material concerns (Matt. 6:25-34). All these texts find parallels in Luke, and three of them (Luke 12:22-31; 12:33-34; 16:13), similarly situated by Luke, likewise treat the same question. We shall examine each of these passages to see what they add to the subject of possessions.

The True Treasure (Matt. 6:19-21)

After three invitations to pursue good works in secret for God alone and not to be seen by others (almsgiving, Matt. 6:1-4; prayer, Matt. 6:5-6; fasting, Matt. 6:16-18—Matthew alone gives these texts), Matthew introduces the text on the true treasure, texts perfectly constructed into antithetic parallels:

19 Do not store up treasures for yourselves on earth, where moths and woodworms destroy them and thieves can break in and steal.
20 But store up for yourselves treasures in heaven, where neither moth nor woodworms destroy them and thieves cannot break in and steal.
21 For where your treasure is, there will your heart be also.

The meaning of these well-phrased sayings is not immediately self-evident. If the heavenly treasures of verse 20 are taken figuratively, what do they refer to? The assurance of divine help in time of material need? Eschatological reward from God? One is advised not to store up treasures on earth or riches (in the proper meaning of the term). Luke's presentation (12:33–34), to which we shall return later, clearly explains that not storing up means selling one's possessions to give alms. This is indeed how one obtains "purses that do not grow old, with a treasure in the heavens that does not fail, where no thief approaches and no moth destroys" (RSV).

Thus, if there were any doubt about Matthew's meaning of earthly treasures (for some,[6] it could be a perishable reputation before others sought by ostentatious good works: almsgiving, prayer, fasting, cf. Matt. 6:1–18), this doubt is dissipated by the comparison with Luke.

The meaning of the first two verses seems, then, to be the following: do not store up perishable riches; rather, ensure for yourselves a treasure, a certain future before God with the life he will give you as a reward. Even though the way to prepare this treasure in heaven is not explicitly indicated by Matthew, we are not mistaken in thinking that for him, as for Luke, it consists of sharing one's possessions with the poorest. "Treasure," in Matthew as in the other Synoptic Gospels, appears precisely in the episode of the rich man invited to sell his possessions to have "a treasure in heaven" (Mark 10:21). The true treasure, then, is the eschatological reward that God reserves for those who do not hold onto riches but, rather, divest themselves to help the needy.

In both Gospels, the pericope ends with a proverb emphasizing the importance of choice. Everyone has a center of gravity where one's full weight is carried; everyone has a treasure on which the heart is set. What is important is to center oneself on true values and not on illusions.

In conclusion let us say that the text of Matthew/Luke presents two teachings related to our subject: one must not store up perishable material riches, which provide no security; true treasure comes from sharing one's possessions with the poor. One is surprised to find here, in parable form, the same message that the Synoptics presented in the episode of the rich man and in the text on the danger of riches (Mark 10:17–31).

The Eye, the Lamp of the Body (Matt. 6:22–23)

Taken by themselves these two verses, among the "most mysterious in the gospel,"[7] seem completely unrelated to the theme of poverty and riches.

22 The lamp of the body is the eye. It follows that if your eye is sound, your whole body will be filled with light.

23 But if your eye is diseased, your whole body will be all darkness. If then, the light inside you is darkness, what darkness that will be!

The comparison with Luke's context or meaning (Luke 11:34–36) is of no help to us. If taken at face value, the image is easy enough to grasp: it is the eye that gives light to the whole body (the person, according to the Semitic expression). The eye must be in a good state (sound); if it is diseased, it will leave the body in darkness. Nevertheless it is not very clear how to apply this teaching. Current exegetical explanations affirm the general truth: if what is central in you (your heart, your intentions) is badly oriented, everything else becomes distorted, warped. In short, your heart is worth what your treasure is. If there is one part of yourself that has not been fully centered on God and his will, your entire being is thrown off balance and is good for nothing.

It is possible that such is the primitive meaning of this obscure logion. But the fact that Matthew has placed it here, after the saying on the treasures and before those on God and money (continuing on the same theme), pushes us to adopt another interpretation. Since the Greek word *haplous* can mean "generous, liberal" (cf. Rom. 12:8; 2 Cor. 8:2; 9:11–13), and since in Hebrew a sound eye signifies kindness, generous almsgiving (Prov. 22:9), the diseased eye would then indicate covetousness and avarice. Through this metaphor Matthew would extend the preceding teaching by inviting the disciple into the liberality that would transform his or her entire being. Otherwise the passage would not apply to the problem of riches and would be out of place in this grouping dedicated precisely to that subject.[8]

The Two Masters (Matt. 6:24)

> No one can serve two masters;
> for either he will hate the one and love the other,
> or he will be devoted to the one and despise the other.
> You cannot serve God and mammon. [RSV]

The first part of this maxim, resembling a popular saying (parallel in Luke, who says, however, "no servant": Luke 16:13), proposes a general truth of common sense: it is impossible for someone to be equally devoted to the service of two masters. It is a wise observation, which can be applied to many situations. In the framework of Jesus' preaching and his challenges it could have been a call to choose, to be aware of one's options, as in the logion, "He who is not with me is against me, and he who does not gather with me scatters" (Matt. 12:30). It is possible that such was Jesus' initial meaning. Matthew concludes with the application of the maxim to God and mammon (a rabbinic expression designating money[9]).

In Luke this text is loosely connected with the parable of the crafty steward (Luke 16:1–12). Its only link with the rest of Matthew's Gospel is the theme of riches.

Clearly the radical choice being offered here is between God and money. Money—here, synonymous with riches—appears as a demanding master absorbing all of one's energies. The recipients of the discourse (in Matthew, Jesus' listeners; in Luke, the disciples) are forewarned that it is impossible to accommodate both; one must choose. The nature of the service (or slavery) to money is not described, nor is the extent to which one can store it up without at the same time "hating or despising" God delineated. But what is clearly affirmed is the sinister shadow of money as a possible rival to God. One recalls the logion mentioned above: "how hard it is for those who have riches to enter into the kingdom of God" (Mark 10:23).

Do Not Be Anxious (Matt. 6:25–34)

This rather long passage (ten verses in Matthew) is, except for a few variants, identical in Matthew/Luke. In Luke it is immediately followed by the previously analyzed text on the true treasure (Luke 12:33–34), which Matthew places at the head of his small anthology.

The articulation of these exhortations is relatively clear. It begins by the invitation not to be anxious, worried, preoccupied with food or clothing. The verb *merimnaô* ("worry") is repeated six times in this passage in Matthew and four times in Luke. We have already encountered it in the parable of the sower (Mark 4:19).

Two arguments support the invitation: Why be anxious about food when the heavenly Father feeds the birds who are of less value than people (v. 26)? Likewise for clothing: Does not God array in splendor the lilies of the fields who are worth less than persons (vv. 28–30)? The reason not to worry is repeated as a conclusion: "Your heavenly Father knows you need them all" (v. 32b). A final sentence condensed the teaching of the entire pericope: "Seek first his kingdom and his righteousness, and all these things shall be yours as well" (RSV).

A few other lines of thinking develop from this theme. First, verse 25 affirms, "Surely life means more than food, and the body more than clothing?" This both complicates the reasoning and deepens it. Then comes verse 27: "Is there a man of you who by anxious thought can add a foot to his height [or, a day to his life]?" (NEB).

This verse demonstrates that these are perfectly useless worries, for one's degree of preoccupation with it cannot add one single cubit to one's stature (increase one's span of life, according to another possible translation). To this verse, Luke adds a commentary (12:26): "If the smallest things, therefore, are outside your control, why worry about the rest?" This can be applied to the question of height, but is less applicable to the span of life (it is no small thing to add to one's lifespan . . .).

At the end of the pericope, Matthew adds a maxim from popular wisdom: "So do not worry about tomorrow: tomorrow will take care of itself. Each day has enough trouble of its own." This somewhat fatalistic proverb must be illumined by what precedes it: each day has its own troubles; it is useless, then, to be anxious about the future, all the more so because God takes care of everyone.

Emerging from this text on anxiousness is, first of all, the centrality of the kingdom, which disciples must seek and to whose demand of justice (Matthew) they must submit. When this concern is truly at the heart of their actions ("first of all," *prôton*), they can surrender with complete trust and faith to the Father who watches over all their needs. This surrender, this absolute trust is another lesson of the text.

There is no mention here of riches. The needs enumerated are elemental and basic: to eat, drink, and clothe oneself. To be anxious about these things is certainly not primarily a problem for the rich but, rather, for the poor. Jesus' instructions remind everyone, the poor as well as the rich, about what the absolute center of one's energies should be. To seek what is essential in life must prevail over the abundance of the rich and the anxieties of the poor.

3. CONCLUSION

The double-tradition texts on possessions analyzed here present less distinctive demands than the previously studied texts. If the Beatitudes proclaim the happiness of the poor (and the unhappiness of the rich), it is, first, because God is on the verge of rescuing them from their distress (material or spiritual, Luke) or, second, because the submissive, the meek (Matthew) already are in the joy of the kingdom.

The Matthean collection (Matt. 6:19–34) and the Lucan parallels are primarily concerned with the necessity of making a choice: the heart must be turned toward the true treasure; the eye must be sound; one must serve only one master; one must seek first of all the kingdom and its justice. By themselves these pieces of advice do not have direct bearing on riches or poverty; rather, they serve as illustrations. However, one finds implicit and occasionally explicit denunciations of certain behavior: riches are false treasure; money is a rival with God; anxiety, even about the basic necessities of life, can impede one's search for the essential. In short, the great lesson which emerges from these texts is a pervasive relativity—of poverty as well as riches—in relation to the choice of God and the kingdom.

It is obvious that, for the evangelists, these instructions (even if Luke 12:22 says "disciples") are addressed to all hearers of the good news, urging them to choose the true treasure and a single master for the sake of the kingdom, which has absolute priority (Matt. 6:3).

A REVIEW OF THE TEXTS

We shall here regroup the texts related to the use of possessions. With the exception of two Matthean texts, they will all be Lucan texts—which are especially abundant, as we have already noted in our presentation.

1. MATTHEW

The Treasure and the Pearl (Matt. 13:44–46)

The two short parables on the hidden treasure and the precious pearl stir in the listener a fascination for the kingdom of God as proclaimed and inaugurated by Jesus. The discovery of its extraordinary value—like a hidden treasure, a priceless pearl—pushes one to sacrifice all in order to possess it. In both cases the steps taken to express this absolute preference for the kingdom consist of selling all that one has in order to purchase it. Strangely enough, "to sell everything" reproduces word for word the expression used by Mark (10:20) and Luke (18:22) in Jesus' demand to the rich man.[10] Does this double parable—whose simplicity and distinctiveness lead us to believe that it is an authentic logion of Jesus—make allusion, beyond the general lesson of preferring the kingdom of heaven over everything, to real actions? In speaking this way Jesus perhaps had some people before him who, in order to follow him, had indeed left and sold everything.

The Last Judgment (Matt. 25:31–46)

In the imposing presentation of the Last Judgment, the Son of man is seated on his throne of glory. He separates the good from the wicked and designates to each group the destiny awaiting them: life or eternal punishment. Jesus' criterion, which determines both the selection and the final destiny, is the exercise of mercy toward the "least of these brothers of mine" (v. 40).

To possess the kingdom prepared since the foundation of the world, a single condition is required—to help those who are in need: the hungry, the thirsty, the stranger, those who are naked, the sick, the prisoners (vv. 35–36). The one who does such services meets the Lord himself in the person of the brother or sister in distress (vv. 40, 45).

This text is the only one in Matthew that affirms the necessity of almsgiving and other works of mercy. In Luke passages of this kind abound. But what is found here has such force and solemnity that the duty of efficacious, fraternal service occupies an absolute and central place. Helping those in need is a basic decisive demand around which everything revolves.

2. LUKE

By far, the most abundant texts on material possessions can be found in Luke. One discovers, first, two important collections (12:13–34; 16:1–31) and then about eight shorter passages without any equivalent in Matthew.

First Grouping (Luke 12:13–34)

This collection includes texts (12:22–34) that Matthew places in a different order in the Sermon on the Mount (Matt. 6:19–21, 25–34). These texts have already been analyzed; here we shall study those peculiar to Luke.

Luke begins with an important declaration. Jesus replies to someone in the crowd who asks him to intervene in a question of inheritance that God has not appointed him as judge of material possessions (Luke 12:13–14). The mere fact of refusal indicates that Jesus' mission is not social or economic; he has neither the capacity nor the power to intervene in this area. What follows is a warning addressed to the crowd (12:15), a transition verse between the episode on inheritance and the parable of the foolish rich man: "Avoid greed in all its forms. A man may be wealthy, but his possessions do not guarantee him life" (NAB).

This recommendation is illustrated by the narrative of the rich man (12:16–21). His land brings in a harvest far greater than what his barn could hold. He then decides to build much larger barns for his surplus in order to lead a life of ease for many years to come, resting, eating, drinking, and celebrating. But God says to him, "Fool! this very night the demand will be made for your soul; and this hoard of yours, whose will it be then?"

The narrative demonstrates, as did verse 15, that one's possessions do not guarantee one's life. The inevitable worries that come with hoarding, the greed, all are vanity, for one is powerless to change the ephermeral character of existence. We perceive in this text a kind of disenchantment echoing the sayings of Qoheleth (Eccles. 2:1–23). Riches are not a guarantee even of life itself.

These maxims of human experience and wisdom take on a more directly religious meaning by the addition of verse 21. "So it is when a man stores up treasure for himself in place of making himself rich in the sight of God." If "making oneself rich" retains its proper meaning, to become rich toward God probably means "to store up treasure for the purpose of providing for the needs of the poor."[11] Thus the stupid rich man of the parable is contrasted with the good rich man who, by giving alms, prepares for himself "purses that do not wear out, treasure that will not fail . . . in heaven" (Luke 12:33).

After Jesus' refusal to intervene in temporal affairs and after the commentary on the vanity of possessions in the face of death, Luke introduces a theme dear to him: riches have meaning only when they are shared. The two subsequent pericopes common to Matthew/Luke (the anxieties about food and clothing, 12:22–31; the true treasure, 12:33–34) have been previously examined (see pp. 77, 80). It suffices here to emphasize what is peculiar to Luke.

One must acknowledge that Luke's order of texts (the warning against covetousness, 12:13–15; the foolish rich man, 12:16–21; the avoidance of worries, 12:13–15; the true treasure, 12:33–34) seems more natural than Matthew's. The argument flows more easily. Following the narrative on the foolish rich man, the warning against anxiety about food and clothing works well even if it seems to apply here especially to the rich. Luke's text of the true treasure is not marked by the perfect parallelism in Matthew: "Do not store up . . . on earth . . . store up in heaven . . . " (Matt. 6:19–20). Matthew's negative invitation is replaced in Luke (12:33) by the radical demand "sell your possessions and give alms." Thus the Lucan equivalent of the imprecise "do not store up . . ." is the peremptory order "sell your possessions." One asks which of the two evangelists modified their common source. In spite of Matthew's perfect construction (because of it, even), it is Luke who seems to have been the most faithful to the original logion. In Matthew the Greek expression for "possessions" (*pôlèsate ta hyparchonta*) is found just as it is in Jesus' invitation to the rich man (Matt. 19:21: *polèson . . . ta hyparchonta*).

In conclusion, there are three places where we encounter in Luke the blunt demand to sell one's possessions: first, in the episode of the rich man (common to the three Synoptics, Mark 10:17-21, see pp. 62-63; Luke 18:22); second, on one of three demands in the collection on renunciation (Luke 14:33, see pp. 54-55); and finally, here in the pericope on the true treasure. In the first and third instances, the final step of selling one's possessions is indicated: giving alms to the poor.

The recipients in the second case were those who heard Jesus, the crowds (14:25). In the third case, the discourse of anxiousness and the treasure (12:22) is addressed to the disciples, although the two preceding passages on greed (12:13-15) and the foolish rich man (12:16-21) were directed at the crowd. Is there an intended distinction or restriction of demand to a particular group? Or is it not, rather, a redactional device indicating a new section? (See Luke 16:1; 17:1, 22.)

The themes of this first Lucan grouping are multiple: Jesus' refusal to intervene in material affairs (vv. 13-14); the warning against greed and hoarding; the impossibility of guaranteeing one's life (vs. 15-20); the uselessness of worries and anxiety, since God takes care of the person; and the priority of God's kingdom (vv. 22-31); the invitation to sell all and give alms, which is the best way of storing up treasure (v. 33).

Second Grouping (Luke 16:1-31)

Two parables—the crafty steward (16:1-9) and the rich man and Lazarus (16:19-31)—serve as the framework of Luke 16 for Jesus' sayings on good and bad uses of money (vv. 9-15). Verses 16 through 18 are an exception and are not related to our theme.

a. The Crafty Steward (Luke 16:1-9). This parable does not present any special difficulties of interpretation, except, perhaps, for the steward's unlikely transactions with the creditors of his master. The latter praises his steward's astuteness; the apparent fraud does not make him indignant because, according to existing Palestinian custom, stewards could consent to loans on their master's possessions and collect a "commission." In the parable, the actual loan on the master's possessions amounted to only fifty measures of oil and a hundred measures of wheat. The remainder seems to have constituted "paying the steward's fees, the exorbitant commission which he had taken for the whole operation."[12] Thus there was no fraud committed against the master; it was the steward who, in order to guarantee his future, deprived himself of an exorbitant and doubtful revenue. In doing so, he exercised foresight; his liberality toward the creditors of his master earned for him their gratitude. Such is the astute behavior of those "of the world" (Luke's commentary).

Jesus then applies the parable to the disciples (v. 9): "And I tell you, make friends for yourselves by means of unrighteous mammon, so that when it fails they may receive you into the eternal habitations" (RSV).

The disciples are told that those who have possessions—designated by a negative connotation: mammon of iniquity, dishonest money—should use them to make friends, no doubt by distributing their riches to the poor. Thus, when money is no longer useful ("when it fails" or, according to another reading of the passage, when you die) you will be received by God in the eternal dwelling place (same expression: 2 Cor. 5:1) of the world to come. This parable indicates to the disciple the paradoxical means of the right use of money: give it to others.

The three verses that follow extend and conclude the lesson given by the parable:

10 He who is faithful in a very little is faithful also in much; and he who is dishonest in a very little is dishonest also in much.
11 If then you have not been faithful in the unrighteous mammon, who will entrust to you the true riches?
12 And if you have not been faithful in that which is another's, who will give you that which is your own? (RSV)

At the origin of this brief discourse, arranged no doubt by Luke, there was in all likelihood one of Jesus' logia, which can be traced to the parable of the talents: the servant faithful in small things is entrusted with greater ones (Matt. 25:21-23; Luke 19:17). This general theme that the one who does well with limited responsibilities will be entrusted with greater ones is applied here to the use of riches. If you cannot be faithful with material riches, who will trust you with the spiritual riches of the kingdom (v. 11)? Verse 12 affirms this by designating the material possessions as being "another's" and the spiritual riches as being the disciples' own possession.

These verses bring nothing that is really new to the parable. They insist on the disciples' duty to use their possessions in the best way possible. The "little," which is "mammon of iniquity" and belongs to "another," must be conscientiously administered —that is, in the vein of the parable's conclusion, used for the service of others, the poor—if the disciple wants to be entrusted with a great good, the life of the kingdom.

Next comes the proverb on the two masters, common to Matthew/Luke, which we have already analyzed (see p. 80). Riches are a perpetual threat, for one cannot serve both God and money.

The two following verses (14-15) are a scathing attack on the hypocrisy of the Pharisees who pass themselves off before others as just. God, however, knowing their hearts, sees their abomination. The same reproach can be read in Matthew 23:28. The only connection of these verses to the theme of riches is Luke's remark that the Pharisees "loved money" (v. 14). A similar idea can be found elsewhere in the Synoptics (at least in Mark/Luke), for example, when Jesus accuses the scribes of being "men who swallow the property of widows" (Mark 12:40). Thus, in Luke, love of money assumes a large place amid the Pharisees' faults.

b. The Rich Man and Lazarus (Luke 16:19-31). Verses 16 to 18 (various pronouncements on the Law, v. 17; divorce, v. 18) interrupt the grouping on possessions. The theme resumes in verse 19 with the parable of the rich man and poor Lazarus (vv. 19-31).

This parable is a marvelous illustration of the wrong use of riches. The rich man is not presented as unjust or oppressive. He is simply a man who used to "dress in purple and fine linen and feast magnificently every day" (v. 19). He is someone to whom the "woe to you" of Luke 6:24 is addressed, because he has already "received his consolation" (RSV). In contrast is the poor man Lazarus; nothing is said about his resignation to his lot or about his virtue, but only his extreme misery is described: lying at the gate, covered with sores and starving. The only thing between the two is a gulf of indifference.

Upon their deaths, however, the situation reverses itself. The poor man is "carried away by the angels to the bosom of Abraham." The rich man is handed over to "torment in Hades" (vv. 22–23).

We need not dwell here on certain traits of the parable, for example, the possible veiled attack against the Sadducees (rich aristocrats of the priestly caste) because of their riches and their refusal of eschatology (they did not believe in angels or the resurrection, Mark 12:18). It suffices for our subject to emphasize that the main lesson is the beatitude of the poor and the malediction of the rich (cf. Luke 6:20, 24), portrayed by Luke as real people. The poor man is comforted and his condition of poverty, starvation, and suffering is totally reversed. The rich man who enjoyed all the advantages during his lifetime is, on the contrary (and because of this), handed over to unhappiness, excluded from life. Although this is not said explicitly, it nonetheless emerges from the fact that he is punished for not discerning how to use his riches, as the crafty steward did, to alleviate the misery of the poor man lying at his gate.

In the dialogue that is initiated between the tormented rich man and Abraham, the question is raised of sending Lazarus back to earth to warn the rich man's five brothers "so that they do not come to this place of torment too" (vv. 27–28). What is this warning if not a reminder of their duty to show concern for the poor and to share with them? Abraham refuses to comply with the impossible request and reaffirms that this duty, extensively proclaimed by Moses and the prophets (see Exod. 22:25; Deut. 24:6, 10–13; Isa. 58:7; Amos 6:4–6; 8:4–7), is sufficiently known; one needs only to listen to them and put what they say into practice.

Let us conclude by saying that Luke's second grouping is completely focused on the use of riches. The parable of the crafty steward (16:1–9) demonstrates the right use of them. It consists of liberal generosity toward others. The three following verses (16:10–12) insist on the necessity of knowing how to administer one's material possessions for this purpose if one wishes to be entrusted with possessions coming from God. Finally, the attack against the Pharisees, lovers of money (16:14–15), prepares one for the parable of the rich man and poor Lazarus, in which the bad use of riches is described (16:19–31). Thus, rather than presenting the demands for radical divestiture, this chapter sharply criticizes wrongly used riches and urges good use of them by sharing with those who have less.

Eight Independent Sayings

What remains to be examined are a certain number of sayings or narratives disseminated throughout Luke and which appear in no distinctive grouping. Some of these passages remotely correspond to ones in Matthew or Mark; others are peculiar to Luke and demonstrate his interest in this theme.

a. *"If anyone has two tunics, he must share" (Luke 3:11).* Luke introduces the concern for sharing in the preaching of John the Baptist. The double tradition (Matt. 3:7–10) emphasizes the blunt character of John's message: the coming wrath; the ax laid to the root of the tree, which even the children of Abraham will not escape unless they change their behavior. Only Luke (3:10–14) adds a concrete development following these warnings. The crowds (Matt. 3:7 mentions only Pharisees and Sadducees), are asked to "bear fruits that befit repentance" (Luke 3:7, RSV), to develop a behavior in accordance with the radical change of life that one henceforth accepts. What will this new behavior be?

In three successive strokes Luke presents the crowds (3:10–11), then the tax collectors (3:12–13), and finally the military (3:14). The behavioral guidelines given to each of these groups reveal Luke's own interests: his sympathy for the despised and rejected classes (the tax collectors: Luke 7:29; 15:1; 18:10–11); his concern for justice and sharing; his moderation.

It is striking to see that the only "fruit of repentance" asked of the crowds is the sharing of material possessions: "If anyone has two tunics he must share with the man who has none, and the one with something to eat must do the same." Are these poor people (to have only two tunics is truly on the border between sufficiency and lack) who are asked to share with those more needy? Or are we faced with a literary expression meaning, "the one who has more should give to the one who has less"? Whatever the case, the basic demand of this new mode of conduct is sharing clothing and food as preached by the Old Testament prophets (Isa. 58:7). That is how real love of neighbor begins; that is true conversion.

b. "Lend without any hope of return" (Luke 6:34–35). In Matthew's pericope on love of enemies (5:43–48), two practical modes of behavior are indicated in addition, of course, to the demand to love. These are prayers for, and greetings to, one's enemies (5:44, 47).

Luke's passage on the same subject (6:27–36), aside from the sayings on nonresistance, which Matthew places in his grouping on the laws of retaliation, shows certain peculiarities that betray his preferences. Thus it is in the teachings on love of enemies that he sets the text on lending.

One must lend without expecting to be reimbursed, for love of one's enemies consists of doing good to them and lending to them without any hope of return (Luke 6:34–35). In Matthew the parallel text is shorter: "Give to anyone who asks, and if anyone wants to borrow, do not turn away" (Matt. 5:42). These sayings, certainly echoes from Jesus' preaching, express a difficult demand: to lend, especially when one expects nothing in return.

c. Give abundantly (Luke 6:30–38). Matthew (5:42) simply says, "Give to anyone who asks." Luke's parallel text (6:30) specifies, "Give [present imperative] to everyone [*panti*] who asks you." Further, Matthew's demand for abstention from judging and condemning (Matt. 7:1) is followed by the criteria for and "measure" of judgment (7:2). Luke, after the same text on judgment, gives the word "measure" a completely material meaning without any relationship to judgment: "Give, and there will be gifts for you: a full measure, pressed down, shaken together, and running over, will be poured into your lap; because the amount you measure out is the amount you will be given back."

This verse is obviously related to the theme of gifts and almsgiving. One must give generously because the promised reward is proportionate (but also without proportions) to the generosity and magnanimity extended to others. Although the end of the verse ("because the amount you measure out") is found in Matthew (7:2) and Mark (4:24), the body of the text is peculiar to Luke, who adds it to his collection of Jesus' sayings on the demands of love. Once again one of these demands is sharing, generous sharing—as much as one would expect from God's infinite generosity.

d. Purification through almsgiving (Luke 11:41). Among the curses that Jesus addresses to the Pharisees and the scribes (derived from a common source that Matthew and Luke arrange each in his own way, Matt. 23:1–36; Luke 11:39–52) is one that denounces the hypocrisy of ritual purity (Matt. 23:25–26; Luke 11:39–41). The scribes and Pharisees are hypocrites because they purify the outside of their cups and plates while the interior is filled with greed and violence. Matthew writes "Blind Pharisees! Clean the inside of the cup and dish first so that the outside may become clean as well" (Matt. 23:26).

Taken in its simple and obvious sense, this logion declares that the rules of ritual purity applied to dishware are worthless if the contents of the dishes were obtained by greed and violence. One must therefore first settle the question of how the goods were obtained. If one is just and does not extort others' possessions (by "devouring" widows' houses, as do the scribes: Mark 12:40; Luke 20:47), then the exterior ritual will take on meaning and truth.

Luke's parallel text, declared by some to be difficult to interpret,[13] seems to have the same basic meaning with a reference typical for Luke on almsgiving. In Luke the contrast is between the outer surface of the dishes (Luke 11:39) and the inner life of the Pharisees (and not the inside of the cup, as in Matthew) who abound with greed and wickedness.

Verse 40 ("Fools! Did not he who made the outside make the inside too?") is an ironic reminder of the basic truth that the God who prescribes the outer rituals of purity is the same who requires interior purity all the more. One can understand, then, verse 41 without great difficulty: "But give for alms those things which are within; and behold, everything is clean for you."

Purifying what is inside the cup (Matt. 23:26)—unjustly acquired possessions—means, according to Luke's text, almsgiving and charity. If the Pharisees, who are "friends of money" (Luke 16:14), want to redeem themselves, purge themselves of their abundant greed and wickedness (Luke 11:39), a means is offered to them: give alms. This text is not unrelated to the teaching on the proper use of "unrighteous mammon" (Luke 16:9). Almsgiving and sharing allow access to the "eternal habitations" (Luke 16:9, RSV) in the life to come. In daily life they take priority over rituals of purity and confer to them their true meaning.

e. Inviting the poor (Luke 14:13, 24). Luke's following three parables are related to a meal: the choice of places (14:7-11); the choice of guests (14:12-14); and the guests who excuse themselves (14:15-24). The last two allude to the poor who must be invited.

In the first case (14:12-14), we find instructions on the choice of guests. When one gives a dinner, one must not invite friends, brothers, parents, or rich neighbors, for fear they might recipro-cate (v. 12). "But when you give a feast, invite the poor, the maimed, the lame, the blind, and you will be blessed, because they cannot repay you. You will be repaid at the resurrection of the just" (RSV).

This text, an invitation to gratuity and detachment regarding earthly things, converges with the teachings of Matthew 5:34-47 and Luke 6:32-35 on charity and love for one's enemies. But here the instructions are applied to kindness toward the poor and the underprivileged.

In the following parable (14:15-24), the great feast, in spite of important differences, is fundamentally the same as Matthew's (Matt. 22:1-14). Luke describes three categories of guests. First are the official guests, for whom the meal had been prepared, who refuse to come (vv. 18-20). Then the master sends the servants with instructions to invite "the poor and maimed and blind and lame" (v. 21). The list is the same as in the preceding text. It is the little ones, gathered from "the streets and alleys of the town," who take the place of those initially invited.

In this parable, which has allegorical traits, the refusal of the good news by the guests (the official leaders of the people: priests, Sadducees, scribes, Pharisees) is due to their material preoccupa-tions with the purchase of land and animals or a recent marriage (Luke 14:18-20). Luke emphasizes the first two more strongly than Matthew (22:5) and adds the excuse of marriage. These are "the riches and pleasures of life" that choke the seed of the Word and prevent it from bearing fruit (Luke 8:14). We see once again how riches and affective bonds can weigh against a choice for the gospel.

On the other hand, in the style of Luke's Beatitudes, the message and the salvation it proclaims (represented here by "a great banquet," Luke 14:16) is offered gratuitously to those who are most poor, socially (the destitute and the crippled) as well as morally (publicans and sinners: see the parables on mercy, Luke 15:1–32). The good news is truly proclaimed to the poor (Matt. 11:5).

f. Renouncing one's possessions (Luke 14:33). This saying, which we have already discussed (see pp. 54–55), is peculiar to Luke and is part of a grouping on renunciation common to Matthew/Luke (Matt. 10:37–39). It is not necessary to analyze it again here, but sufficient to note that Luke repeats it in equivalent form two other times: in the narrative of the rich man (Luke 18:22) and in the teaching on the true treasure (Luke 12:33).

This insistence on such an absolute demand is indicative of Luke's main concerns. For him this is the important point of Jesus' teaching, and he does not bother to use nuance, at least in this immediate context.

We have said previously that the saying "renounce all" was a Lucan creation (see pp. 54–55). This is true of the collection in Luke (14:25–33). But a question arises concerning the source of this apparently general demand of renouncing all one's possessions (Luke 14:33) and selling them for almsgiving (Luke 12:33; 18:22). One can imagine a number of hypotheses: (1) a pure and simple creation by Luke; (2) a communal creation preserved by Luke and omitted by or unknown to Matthew/Mark; or (3) a radical saying of Jesus, transmitted by the community and retained with emphasis by Luke. Although no compelling answer emerges, it is nonetheless difficult to accept the first two hypotheses. How could one imagine the community or the evangelist creating a demand addressed to all ("the crowds," Luke 14:25) which was never put into practice by the disciples as a whole? That seems even less probable when one considers that Luke is not alone; the Synoptic tradition has maintained the same demand in the episode of the rich man (see pp. 62–69). One can then reasonably assume that Jesus himself is the source of such a radical statement: the rich cannot enter into the kingdom unless they renounce their possessions. The presence of well-to-do people among Jesus' friends (Martha and Mary, Luke 10:38; women "who provided for him out of their own resources," Luke 8:3; Mark 15:41;

Joseph of Arimathea, Matt. 27:57) excludes a literal and legalistic interpretation of this demand but does not invalidate it, especially since these few figures are presented in the very act of giving and sharing.[14]

g. *Zacchaeus (Luke 19:1–10).* In this episode Luke narrates the conversion of a man belonging to a class abhorred and despised by the scribes and the Pharisees (Luke 15:2). He was a publican, a collector of Roman taxes, a rich unjust collaborator. We need to see what happens to a rich man when Jesus' call takes hold of him.

We must note that Jesus does not address this man with any special call to follow or to sell his possessions. He simply invites himself into the house of a man who, by reason of his trade and his wealth, is considered a sinner (Luke 19:7).

Zacchaeus' first action following the joyous welcome (which indicates the change in him, his conversion) is his spontaneous and generous sharing. "Look, sir, I am going to give half my property to the poor" (v. 8a). Then comes the restitution: "and if I have cheated anybody, I will pay him back four times the amount" (v. 8b).

To offer restitution is only right, but Zacchaeus goes beyond the measure imposed by the Law.[15] In his initial decision one finds once again the action we have encountered many times in Luke (and in the narrative of the rich man, Mark 10:17–27) of giving one's possessions to the poor. Certainly it is only half of his possessions, but Luke is not emphasizing a particular amount but, rather, generosity and gratuity. There is a joyous atmosphere in this narrative: salvation is available. Sharing grows and riches are cast off—not out of asceticism or guilty conscience but in a joyful move toward one's neighbor. This episode about Zacchaeus makes two points. On the one hand, salvation, conversion, and joy are incompatible with the burden of riches. We rediscover here one of Luke's constant preoccupations: the kingdom and riches are counteractive. On the other hand, Luke demonstrates, if this is necessary, that a gift cannot be calculated mathematically. Half of one's possessions does not indicate a limit but emphasizes Zacchaeus' magnanimity and the prodigality of the gift.[16] It is not so much a question of the quantity given by this rich man converted to the gospel but the heartfelt generosity and joy with which he gives.

We have in Zacchaeus the counterpart to Luke's rich man (16:19–31) imprisoned by his wealth and comfort. The prison wall has fallen for Zacchaeus, for his wealth has become a source of joy for others.

h. The widow's mite (Luke 21:1–4). This text is one of the rare passages common to Mark/Luke but absent in Matthew (Mark 12:41–44). A contrast is made between the Temple offerings of rich people who put in "large sums" (Mark 12:41, RSV) and the offering of a poor widow ("poverty-stricken," Luke 21:2) who puts in only "two small coins." Of itself this offering is ridiculous; yet "this poor widow has put in more than any of them; for . . . she has put in all she had to live on" (vv. 3–4).

What is involved here is not detachment or sharing but a gesture of cultic generosity. If the poor widow is praised, it is because of the totality of the gift; she gives her all to the Temple, even if it is out of proportion with the offerings of the rich. What counts for Jesus is not the material quantity but the generosity of heart. The rich give only out of their abundance (21:4). The generosity of the poor is total.

The teaching of this passage does not bear directly on wealth or poverty. It magnifies true generosity and criticizes the pretense of it. True, the poor widow is cast in the good role, while the rich appear pretentious. And yet, whether it is the widow who gives "all that she has to live on" or Zacchaeus who gives only half of his possessions, the movement is identical. The giving is meant to be total.

Conclusion

The eight passages in Luke that have just been examined repeat already encountered themes, concretize them, and apply them. Among these texts are, seemingly, logia of Jesus that were transported by the tradition common to Matthew/Luke, which Luke alone preserved (notably the texts in sections *b, c, d, f*). The designation of the poor (text, section *e*) may be a later redactional addition. The episode about Zacchaeus, even though it betrays Luke's flourishes and preoccupation, must contain a kernel of ancient historical fact.

In these texts we read the blunt demand of renouncing everything if one wants to be a disciple of Jesus (Luke 14:33). Other passages insist on the necessity of almsgiving if one wants to be truly pure (Luke 11:41); of giving abundantly (Luke 6:38); of lending and expecting nothing in return (Luke 6:34–35); and of inviting into one's home those who cannot reciprocate (Luke 14:13–24). The text on the poor as the privileged beneficiaries of salvation (Luke 14:21) echoes the Beatitude on poverty. Finally, the episodes of Zacchaeus (Luke 19:1–10) and the poor widow (Luke 21:1–4) each illustrate the necessity of giving and sharing with total generosity.

None of the texts seems to be reserved for a limited circle of hearers. Except for the challenges to the Pharisees (Luke 11:41), they are addressed to Jesus' general audience and the readers of the Gospels.

The underlying motives for the proposed conduct are pure gratuity in God's image (Luke 6:35–36), the hope of reward at the resurrection (Luke 14:14), which will be given in abundance (Luke 6:38), and finally, the desire for true purity in the eyes of God (Luke 11:40–41). What motivated Zacchaeus to distribute half of his possessions to the poor was the coming of salvation to his house in the person of Jesus, Savior of the lost (Luke 19:9–10).

GENERAL CONCLUSION

In relationship to the preceding chapters on discipleship (chap. 3) and renunciation (chap. 4), this one is considerably more extensive. This is because the texts examined here were more numerous (sixteen texts in chap. 5 as opposed to twelve in chap. 3 and three in chap. 4), often longer, and the analyses more detailed. We can only hope that nothing of importance escaped us.

Is this to say that this theme—attitudes toward possessions—constitutes a pole of thought more important than others? At any rate, what obviously emerges is that this problem preoccupied the Christian generation that witnessed the birth of the Gospels. Facts and sayings of Jesus were preserved and used differently by the redactors. Even though Luke's material on this theme far exceeds what the other evangelists transmit, the fact remains that the essence of what he says is explicitly affirmed in the Synoptic grouping (Mark 10:17–31) and repeated in passages common to Matthew (6:19–34). These texts proclaim that one must divest oneself of possessions to share them with the poor and that wealth is an insurmountable obstacle to salvation. Texts found elsewhere in the double tradition and those peculiar to Luke repeat and enrich the various harmonics of this primary demand.

What points emerge from the texts analyzed in this chapter? In my opinion they can be grouped around two poles: (1) the judgment on material possessions and (2) the invitation, the command to sell everything in order to share.

The possessions that one owns are never qualified as evil in themselves. However, by designating them as "unrighteous mammon" (Luke 16:9–11) derived from injustice and greed (Luke 11:39), Luke clearly demonstrates the negative connotations. They are, at any rate, a source of anxiety and worry (Matt. 6:25–34) and a deception or a seduction (Mark 4:19); one quickly becomes enslaved by them (Matt. 6:24). They also choke the Word (Mark 4:10) and prevent one from seeking the kingdom (Matt. 6:33), responding to the invitation to the feast (Luke 14:18–20), and serving God (Matt. 6:24). They become a false treasure (Matt. 6:19–21). The security that the rich think possessions afford proves deceptive and fragile; they offer no security against death (the foolish rich man, Luke 12:16–21). Riches constitute an insurmountable obstacle to salvation (apologue of the camel, Mark 10:23–27). It is because the rich man unconsciously used them for himself alone that he was thrown in the place of torments and his five brothers were threatened with the same fate (Luke 16:19–31). Jesus' instructions are an invitation not to be anxiously preoccupied with these possessions, or even life's essentials (Matt. 6:25–34). God alone must be served and trusted (Matt. 6:24–25) by setting one's heart where the true treasures are (Matt. 6:21).

All the texts describe the perils of material possessions. Luke, however, is the only one to report examples and sayings demonstrating that it is possible to use them properly. This was the case for (1) the Pharisees ("lovers of money," Luke 16:14, RSV), who, by giving alms (Luke 11:41), could have made everything pure, even their possessions obtained from extortion and wickedness; (2) the crafty steward, who won the trust of his creditors (Luke 16:1–9); and (3) Zacchaeus, who gave half of his possessions to the poor and made restitution four times over the amount of his unjust profits (Luke 19:1-10). One needs only to learn from the crafty steward praised by the Lord (Luke 16:10-12).

The second pole—the invitation or demand to sell one's possessions—is powerfully affirmed in the exemplary episode of the rich man (Mark 10:17-22), common to the Synoptics. The Synoptic tradition, as well as the double tradition, does not return to this theme, though Matthew perhaps alludes to it in the parables of the treasure and the pearl of the kingdom (Matt. 13:44-45). Luke, however, repeats the command twice (Luke 12:33; 14:33). He insists on the generosity that must animate this deed: one must give abundantly (Luke 6:30, 38), without expecting anything in return (Luke 6:34-35; 14:13), as Zacchaeus (Luke 19:1-10) and the poor widow (Luke 21:1-4) did. Let us note that this divestiture is always related to sharing with the poor (Luke 14:33 is an exception). One divests oneself of possessions in order to distribute the proceeds to the poor (Mark 10:21) and to give alms (Luke 12:33). The right use of riches is charity, as Zacchaeus' gesture demonstrates. One divests oneself for love of others and to help them.

It is astonishing that, except for the Beatitude on the poor (Matt. 5:3), these texts do not directly address poverty. Possessions and sharing are mentioned; riches are dangerous; one must know how to use them. The poor are proclaimed blessed (in Luke), but only because their poverty is at its end, for they have been invited to the feast (Luke 14:13) and, like Lazarus, are resting in the bosom of Abraham (Luke 16:22). Paradoxically, even Luke, called "the evangelist of the poor,"[17] speaks more about material possessions, their danger and their usage, than about the poor and poverty.

The analyses of this chapter again demonstrate that the recipients of these teachings and demands are not the limited group of disciples. Some doubt may remain about the case of the rich man. Nevertheless, all the other texts are addressed to the whole of Jesus' audience (disciples, the crowd, everyone) and to the hearers and readers of the Word.

The motivations for such radical behavior are, as we have seen, diverse. It is "for the sake of Jesus" (Mark 10:29), and out of desire to become his disciple, which one cannot be without renouncing all that one owns (Luke 14:33; cf. also Mark 10:21). The motivation of a reward appears also: to obtain eternal life and a treasure in heaven, the rich man must sell all (Mark 10:17, 21); those who have left everything will receive a hundredfold (Mark 10:30); those who give will receive an overflowing measure (Luke 6:38) and will be welcomed into the eternal dwelling places (Luke 16:9) at the time of the resurrection (Luke 14:14). They will have a treasure in heaven (Mark 10:21; Matt. 6:21). Finally, the most immediate motivation for abandoning possessions is almost always sharing with the poor (Mark 10:21; Luke 12:33). For Zacchaeus it seems to flow from the joy of having received salvation (Luke 19:9).

NOTES

1. This passage receives a thorough examination in the book on the subject by S. Légasse, *L'appel du riche* (Paris: Beauchesne, 1966), p. 204.

2. Braun, *Spätjüdisch—häretischer und früchristlicher Radikalismus*, 2 vols. (Tübingen: J. C. B. Mohr, 1969), 2:76, n. 1, and Schulz, *Nachfolgen und Nachame* (Munich: Kösel, 1962), p. 77, n. 40, hold the opposite opinion: the *teleios* is an expression of a double ethic—the ordinary way of salvation vs. perfection.

3. A good analysis of this pericope is found in Paul Minear, *Commands of Christ* (Nashville: Abingdon, 1972), pp. 106–9.

4. To unravel the meaning of the Beatitudes, the study of J. Dupont, *Les Béatitudes*, Études Bibliques (Paris: Gabalda, 1969), 3:204, was very helpful.

5. Dupont, *Béatitudes*, p. 470.

6. P. Bonnard, *L'Évangile selon Saint Matthieu* (Neuchâtel: Delachaux et Niestlé, 1970), p. 90.

7. Ibid.

8. For the interpretation of this pericope we follow the opinions of Boismard, *Synopse de quatre évangiles en français*, 2 vols. (Paris: Cerf, 1972), 2: 277–78.

9. See Braun, *Spätjüdisch* 2:74, n. 3; 2:77, n. 2.

10. Légasse, "L'appel du riche," resumé article in *La pauvreté évangélique,* Lire la Bible, 27 (Paris: Cerf, 1971), p. 70.

11. Boismard, *Synopse*, 2:281.

12. Ibid., 2:296

13. Manson, *The Sayings of Jesus* (London: SCM Press, 1971), p. 269.

14. Braun, *Spätjüdisch*, 2:76, n. 1.

15. In cases of restitution, one was required to add one-fifth the value of the object (Lev. 5:24).

16. Passages with the same meaning: "I will give you half my kingdom": Herod to the daughter of Herodias, Mark 6:23; cf. also Esther 5:3.

17. This is the name that H. J. Degenhardt gives him in the title of his book: *Lukas—Evangelist der Armen* (Stuttgart: Kath. Bibelwerk, 1965).

6

The Radicalization of the Law

This chapter will examine Matthew's great inaugural discourse, usually called the Sermon on the Mount (Matt. 5:1–7:27). In this collection of instructions derived from the double tradition and especially from sources peculiar to Matthew—a collection structured as a coherent whole—Matthew presents God's new justice (Matt. 5:20; 6:1).

The kingdom of God inaugurated by Jesus introduces demands far more extensive and deep than those of the old Law. These demands radicalize exterior behavior and unmask the secret intentions of the heart. For this reason the discourse may be said to constitute a charter of Christian radicalism.

Some parts of this long text have already been presented in the preceding chapter's examination of possessions (see pp. 75–83). Our analysis here obliges us to extend the concept of radicalism. Denying oneself, breaking family ties, and divesting oneself in order to base one's life on trust and begin sharing—aspects studied above—are not the extent of radical conduct. It is also an attitude of humility, gentleness, peace, and mercy (the Beatitudes, Matt. 5:3–12); it is a new type of relationship excluding anger, vengeance, exploitation of others and including love of enemies, the respect of commitments, loyalty, honesty (the six antitheses, Matt. 5:21–48). It is, finally, the intention of pleasing God alone in one's good deeds (Matt. 6:1–18). Under these conditions, disciples hungry and thirsty for justice (Matt. 5:6), a justice extending beyond that of the scribes and the Pharisees (Matt.

5:20), will be perfect as their heavenly Father is perfect (Matt. 5:48) and will be able to enter the kingdom of heaven (Matt. 5:20).

THE RADICALISM OF THE BEATITUDES

While commenting on the Beatitudes of the poor in Luke's version, we have summarily indicated the two most important problems concerning the Beatitudes in general: (1) differences of number and meaning between the two versions (Matthew/ Luke) and (2) the Beatitudes' original meaning (see pp. 75–77). A messianic manifesto, the Beatitudes proclaim a reversal in favor of the poor, the starving, the afflicted and, later on, the persecuted Christians who will be freed and filled with happiness. These blessings and felicitations do not delineate modes of conduct but, rather, conditions of injustice which God, in his sovereign justice through the intermediary of his messenger Jesus, was preparing himself to abolish. In this sense the Beatitudes as Jesus could have pronounced them and as Luke, with modifications, presented them are not related to what we mean by radicalism in this study. We find something different in Matthew and it is on this version that we need to dwell.

1. THE BEATITUDES ACCORDING TO MATTHEW (MATT. 5:3–12)

Matthew adds five Beatitudes to Luke's four. He divides in two the Beatitude of the poor; "gentle" (or "humble": *praeis*) of the second Beatitude (v. 4) carries a meaning close to that of "the poor in spirit." Likewise the eighth ("Happy those who are persecuted in the cause of right," v. 10) seems to anticipate and condense in a Matthean perspective the last blessing: "Happy are you when people abuse you and persecute you" (v. 11). To these two pairs Matthew adds three new Beatitudes: the merciful (v. 7), the pure in heart (v. 8), the peacemakers (v. 9).

Besides numerical additions, the addition of a few words modifies the Beatitudes that Matthew has in common with Luke. Thus the poor become the "poor in spirit" (*en pneumati*, v. 3); the hungry become those who "hunger and thirst for justice" (v. 6); those who weep are designated as those who "mourn" (*penthountes*, v. 5); and the persecuted suffer "for the sake of justice"

(v. 10). The clearest modification concerns those who hunger. In Luke those who are physically hungry constitute one of three categories of people in distress. To be hungry and thirsty for the sake of justice, in Matthew's language, means to desire ardently and to live concretely according to the new justice—that is, according to the demands expounded in the Sermon on the Mount. It is no longer a question of misery but an interior disposition.

Adding "in spirit" to the Beatitude of the poor introduces the same kind of change. It is no longer the poor in the sociological sense but those who have the "spirit" (or the soul) of a poor person. Concurring with the exegesis of Dom Dupont, which seems the most solidly based, we believe that "the qualification 'in spirit' is not only meant to add something to the idea of exterior poverty; it calls for a total transposition."[1] The poor in spirit are those who are bowed down and who humbly submit, enduring everything with gentle patience.[2] One must resemble a child to enter the kingdom (only Matt. 18:3).

Matthew's Beatitudes describe an inner attitude (the merciful forgive and are kind; the pure in heart conform to God's will; the peacemakers desire concrete peace and reconciliation). They force us to interpret the entire discourse in the same perspective. Matthew is not describing a situation but delineating a mode of conduct. He is proposing to the Christians of his time a way of living that flows from a new situation, and this way of living is radical.

2. THE DEMANDS OF THE BEATITUDES

Thus the Matthean Beatitudes specify how the disciples must live if they want to enjoy the happiness already given and yet still promised. Without dwelling on these images of happiness, which, while now filling the disciple's heart, turn him or her toward the eschatological future, we shall look more closely at the attitudes proposed by the texts and their radical character.

The texts present certain requirements regarding one's attitude toward God and one's neighbor. Those who mourn (v. 5), who hunger and thirst for justice (v. 6), and the pure of heart (v. 8) essentially portray a certain way of being before God. Those who mourn, as in Matthew's context, are not merely those in need or distress or repentant sinners. They are, rather, those who are mourning over the present situation of the world, which is under the forces of evil, suffering, and death. They suffer over the unfulfilled promises of the kingdom and await the God of consolation who will come when the kingdom is inaugurated.

Those who hunger for justice ardently pursue and desire a living justice—that is, the integral fulfillment of the will of God. They want to be disciples and Christians in the fullest sense. The Beatitude of the pure in heart comes close in meaning: the pure in heart act "in conformity to the will of God; such conduct assumes a conversion of heart, an authentic inner submission and perfect integrity toward God."[3] Purity of heart is perfect loyalty and perfect sincerity toward God.

Three Beatitudes concentrate on the behavior toward one's neighbor: the gentle (v. 4), the merciful (v. 7), the peacemakers (v. 9). Like Jesus, who was "gentle and humble in heart" (Matt. 11: 29), the gentle disciple is "tranquil, peaceful—the opposite of those who lose their temper and are violent. He endures opposition, is without aggressivity, and avoids quarrels." That gentleness is "a form of charity, patient and carefully attentive to the needs of others."[4]

The merciful forgive others (Matt. 6:12, 14-15), following God's example; they abstain from judging and condemning (Matt. 7:1-2), and are helpful and kind to all those in need, as expressed in the parable of judgment (Matt. 25:31-46).

The peacemakers (*eirenopoioi*) undertake another form of works of mercy. They wish to bring peace by reconciling those divided by discords or quarrels. "They love peace enough not to fear compromising their own personal peace by intervening in conflicts in order to bring peace where there is division."[5] In so doing, they are actively engaged in the service of their brothers and sisters, which Matthew's discourse makes explicit.

The Beatitudes of "the poor in spirit" (v. 3) and the two Beatitudes of the persecuted constitute a separate category. The first is related to God and neighbor. The poor in spirit are not, as is generally believed, those "interiorly detached from the money they possess or lack."[6] Rather, they are the humble who lower themselves and become interiorly like little ones, like children (Matt. 18:3), before God and their neighbor. This spiritual poverty (in Matthew this is unrelated to material poverty) requires the disciple to be humble in heart, dependent on God and others, and the servant of all.

The two Beatitudes about the persecuted (vv. 10–11) as found in Luke are closest to the original meaning. They address outer situations and not dispositions of the heart. One is not persecuted out of choice or desire, but rather, one undergoes persecution. Even here, however, Matthew introduces his special concern: the ones who are persecuted are not to be congratulated merely because they have suffered persecution, but rather, because they are striving to live the new justice taught and required by Jesus. Thus what is blessed is ultimately an attitude: to live according to the new justice, even when it sparks persecution, is happiness.

3. CONCLUSION

Matthew's Beatitudes paint the portrait of the ideal disciples. Those who are happy, blessed by God, and promised future happiness ardently strive to live (hunger and thirst for) the justice of the kingdom and act with integrity and purity (the pure in heart). They suffer (mourn) when seeing the world and themselves far from such justice, but rest assured that this situation will be changed by God.

Thus they stand humbly before God and others (the poor in heart). Full of gentleness and patience, ready to endure anything (the gentle), they give themselves to serving others actively. They avoid judging others and instead forgive them and help them with their own resources (the merciful), intervening in the midst of conflicts and divisions to reestablish peace (the peacemakers). And if, because of such conduct, they are slandered in every way and persecuted, they will consider themselves blessed (the persecuted).

Compared to normal social conduct, we see how paradoxical such behavior is. It thoroughly upsets the ordinary patterns of thinking and acting. "To do justice, and to love kindness, and to walk humbly with your God . . ." (Mic. 6:8, RSV) is the program which Matthew announces at the very beginning of the Sermon on the Mount and which he develops in the texts that follow.

"BE PERFECT": THE SIX ANTITHESES

After the Beatitudes (Matt. 5:3–11), and after the two images of Jesus' disciples being "the salt of the earth" (5:13) and "the light of the world" (5:14–16), the Sermon on the Mount presents a series of six juxtaposing antitheses (5:21–48). This series begins by the contrasting declaration "You have heard that it was said. . . . But I say to you . . ." (RSV). To the oft-quoted Law (the Torah), Jesus juxtaposes his own demands, which abolish this Law or at least go far beyond it.

This important grouping obviously raises many historico-critical questions. What was the form and content of Jesus' teachings transcending the Law? What was the communal and redactional contribution to how these antitheses were to be presented? Finally, the basic question arises: Is there really and invariably something "extra" above and beyond the demands of the Law?

Without going into detail of all the multiple and contradictory exegetical answers available, we can indicate the point where general agreement exists.[7] Although the literary arrangement is Matthew's, the basis, in many cases, is primitive and connects with Jesus' teachings—teachings sometimes returning to the very sources of the Law to contradict the interpretations of the scribes and the Pharisees (for example, Matt. 15:1–9; 19:1–6) and at other times going beyond the Law.

Whatever the case, the emphasis of this collection is indicated by the introductory verses on the Law that Jesus came not to abolish but to fulfill (v. 17), and on the disciples' justice, which must surpass that of the scribes and the Pharisees (v. 20; repeated in the final verse calling the disciples to be perfect as their heavenly Father is perfect, v. 48). Framed by such an introduction (vv. 17–20) and conclusion (v. 48), the antitheses clearly indicate what is at stake: the justice proposed by Jesus calls a person to a complete reorientation. Our examination of the antitheses will demonstrate the extent of the demands.

1. KILLING AND ANGER (MATT. 5:21–26)

The first antithesis compares killing and anger. This opposition is clearly and simply expressed in the first two phrases:

21   You have heard that it was said to the men of old, "you shall not kill; and whoever kills shall be liable to judgment."

22a   But I say to you that every one who is angry with his brother shall be liable to judgment [RSV].

The verses that follow extend and develop the concise statement of verses 22a. Thus in verse 22b and c two kinds of insults are included with anger, followed by increasingly serious punishments:

22b   if a man calls his brother "Fool" [*raqa*: empty-head, nitwit] he will answer for it before the Sanhedrin;

22c   and if a man calls him "Renegade" he will answer for it in hell fire.

A dilemma follows: what is more important, to present an offering to the Temple or to reconcile oneself with one's brother? Jesus declares: leave your offering before the altar and first go be reconciled with your brother (vv. 23–24). Verses 25 and 26, which have their parallel in Luke (12:57–59), insist on the necessity of reconciling oneself as soon as possible with one's adversary.

The first two verses form the antithesis and are directly related to our subject of transcending the Law. Paradoxically what is affirmed is that somehow murder and anger are equally serious crimes. The first results in judgment (and condemnation) and the second entails similar consequences. The judgments and condemnations gradually increase—an ordinary tribunal, the tribunal of the Sanhedrin (the Jewish supreme court), the divine tribunal ("the fires of Gehenna," NAB)—to orchestrate the idea that anger, and all that accompanies it, is as pernicious and as damnable as murder.

Although we already find in wisdom literature a warning against anger (Sir. 28:11), this antithesis is a new one because it addresses both inner anger and its outer manifestation. To the Fifth Commandment forbidding murder, Jesus opposes his own law, which condemns even bad feelings toward others.

2. ADULTERY AND EVIL DESIRE (MATT. 5:27-32)

The Sixth Commandment forbids adultery (Exod. 20:14). Jesus declares (Matt. 5:28), "But I say this to you: if a man look at a woman lustfully, he has already committed adultery with her in his heart."

To this connection between desire and action, Matthew adds an exhortation on the radical treatment needed to rectify the scandal caused by part of the body: tear out the eye or cut off the hand (Matt. 5:29-30). In context, this demand obviously means that to avoid sinning one should sacrifice everything—specifically, the impure covetousness that wrongs one's neighbor. We shall return to this text, which is encountered two other times (Matt. 18:8-9; Mark 9:43-48) and whose primary meaning seems more general than Matthew's application here.

Let us note again that the connection between desire and action and the equal condemnation of both, though remotely parallel to other Bible passages (interdiction of coveting another's wife, Exod. 20:17b; of looking upon her lustfully, Sir. 9:5-8; Job 31:1, 9) and sayings in contemporary Judaism, were never strictly affirmed. Here again Jesus' teaching uncovers the intentions of the heart and denounces the very source of evil.

Although this second antithesis seems to emphasize one's inner disposition, it is not unrelated to the neighbor. It forbids turning women into objects, and by forbidding the act and even the desire for adultery it protects the bond of justice that unites men and women.

3. EXCLUSION OF DIVORCE (MATT. 5:31-32)

31 It has also been said: Anyone who divorces his wife must give her a writ of dismissal.

32 But I say this to you: everyone who divorces his wife, except for the case of fornication, makes her an adulteress; and anyone who marries a divorced woman commits adultery.

Jesus' declaration on divorce can be found in this juridical form twice in Matthew (here and 19:9), once in Mark (10:11–12) and once in Luke (16:18). The exclusion of divorce is reaffirmed in Mark/Matthew, where the notion of God's original plan is developed (Mark 20:2–9). Paul seems to be referring to the latter in 1 Corinthians 7:10.

The exegetes are unanimous on the fact that this absolute interdict correcting the Mosaic Law must come from Jesus himself.[8] The format in Mark 10:2–9 seems to preserve the original meaning. The more juridical formulation, which applies a specific prohibition to a concrete situation, could be of communal origin. Luke has the simplest form (Luke 16:18): "Everyone who divorces his wife and marries another is guilty of adultery, and the man who marries a woman divorced by her husband commits adultery."

Presenting this declaration with an antithesis is Matthew's setting. It is even probable that he added it to the five other antitheses in his Gospel. The evangelist thus wanted to demonstrate how Jesus' teaching on the indissolubility of marriage not only transcends but contradicts and abrogates the law authorizing divorce (Deut. 24:14).

It is true that Matthew introduces a clause that seems to reduce considerably the radicality of the new law: "except for the case of fornication" (5:32; same exception in 19:9). We must note first that the designated case is described not as adultery, for which there is a specific word, *moicheia*, but as *porneia* (a vague term meaning lewd conduct, prostitution). There are conflicting interpretations on the nature of this exception. Is it a woman's lewd conduct, that is to say, adultery, which authorizes divorce? Some exegetes think so, forgetting how unlikely it is that the community would modify an absolute rule of Jesus. Others are of the opinion (which seems more solid) that the Judeo-Christian community gave authorization to break up those unions which under Jewish law are illegitimate (Lev. 18:6–18), considering them as *porneia*. This position would be confirmed by Acts 15:20, 29 where *porneia* designated, in all likelihood, illegitimate unions. Finally, the separation of spouses, without allowing for remarriage—a truly unknown phenomenon in Jewish circles—is not unthinkable, since even Paul considers it (1 Cor. 7:11).[9]

Whatever the interpretation of this brief clause, Jesus' original thought on divorce is clear. Even more than in the preceding case the radicalism of his demands is striking. The indissolubility of conjugal bonds, which is traced to the will of the Creator (Mark 10:6–9), is a demand that startles even Jesus' disciples. It more than transcends, it reverses the old Law. Men and women are invited to meet the test of mutual fidelity—a fidelity rooted in God's plan for their lives.

4. OATH-TAKING (MATT. 5:33–37)

The Law forbade bearing false witness (Exod. 20:16) and swearing falsely (Lev. 19:12). In Matthew's fourth antithesis Jesus forbids all oath-taking (Matt. 5:34; see an important parallel in Jas. 5:12) and demands that one's word be clear and simple: a yes, yes; a no, no (Matt. 5:37).

But the passage is not that simple, for other themes intervene to complicate it. The interdict on perjury is taken from Psalm 50:14 and appears here in verse 33: "You must not break your oath, but must fulfill your oaths to the Lord." The essence of the antithesis is very clear: "But I say this to you: do not swear at all."

Nevertheless, the following verses (34b–36), by themselves, do not seem to exclude all oaths absolutely but only certain forms of oath-taking, such as those that take God as witness (parallel: Matt. 23:20–22):

34b either by heaven, for it is the throne of God,
35 or by the earth, for it is his footstool, or by Jerusalem, for it is the city of the great king [RSV].

Excluded are individuals swearing upon themselves, since one cannot even be one's own master: "Do not swear by your own head either, since you cannot turn a single hair white or black" (v. 36). The final verse (37) declares that one's answer must be simple and truthful: "All you need say is 'Yes' if you mean yes, 'No' if you mean no; anything more than this comes from the evil one."

Is the evangelist simply affirming that what one says should be true (the yes must truly be a yes; the no, truly no, without lies or dissimulation, as Jas. 5:12 says), or is Matthew adopting the custom known to Jews of an undivided Yes or No acting as an oath? It is not easy to settle this question.

As we have previously seen, the interdict of all oath-taking and the reminder to speak simply and honestly constitute the essence of this passage, which extends deeper than the Law and Jewish practice (with the exception of the Essenes)[10] and can no doubt be traced back to Jesus.

Regardless of appearances, the message here is about interpersonal relationships. One must exclude all appeals to God, his substitutes (heaven, earth, Jerusalem), and even the most precious part of the body—the head—because ultimately one's word must be rediscovered in its transparent honesty. Only then can men and women trust what is affirmed or denied without having to invoke outside (even divine) guarantees.

5. RESISTING EVIL (MATT. 5:8-42)

The *lex talionis* ("Law of retaliation") of Exodus 21:22–25 regulated and curtailed excessive acts of vengeance by imposing a punishment equal to (and not greater than) the offense. "Eye for eye and tooth for tooth" (Matt. 5:38) meant a punishment equal to the injury received. In relation to this prescription, Jesus declares something truly unheard of in his fifth antithesis: "But I say to you, do not resist one who is evil. But if anyone strikes you on the right cheek, turn to him the other also" (v. 39, RSV).

The transcendence here is total. Far from requiring exacting preparation, even within bonds, the disciple must submit him- or herself (almost actively) to the evil one by offering the cheek that has not yet been struck. The same exorbitant demand is expressed in verse 41: "Should anyone press you into service for one mile, go with him two miles" (NAB).

To "press into service" is a technical term for forced labor imposed by the Roman military authority probably to transport goods. To fulfill these duties the disciple is required, paradoxically, to double the required amount of work and do so without grumbling. This task is all the more repugnant, since it is ordered by an "evil one," as verse 39 says. Three other examples are given:

40 if a man takes you to law and would have your tunic, let him have your cloak as well.

42 Give to anyone who asks, and if anyone wants to borrow, do not turn away.

These three cases as well as the rest of the logion on turning the other cheek (v. 39b) have corresponding verses in Luke (6:29–30). One notices different attitudes in the last two examples. It is not a spirit of nonresistance to evil, ill-treatment, or force, but a spirit of generous giving. This demonstrates, once more, the composite character of the collection. Nonetheless, what is clear is the revolutionary, radical nature of the proposals. Even while allowing for literary paradox, we must acknowledge that Jesus establishes a mode of conduct that goes against the grain of the Law and human behavior.

6. LOVE YOUR ENEMIES (MATT. 5:43–48)

43 "You have heard that it was said, 'You shall love your neighbor and hate your enemy.'

44 But I say to you, love your enemies and pray for those who persecute you. . ." [RSV].

This sixth and last antithesis, which clearly and simply expresses Jesus' incredible call to transcend oneself, presents no difficulty of interpretation. These two verses constitute Matthew's central point: the love of neighbor extends beyond one's circle of friends and relatives to encompass even those who do not want to be one's neighbor.

The phrase of verse 43, "hate your enemy," raises at least two problems. First, neither the Scriptures nor Jewish tradition (apart from Qumran)[11] contains such a formula. Both do express "the principle of love of enemies . . . but not in such a strong way"[12] as Jesus does and with exceptions (cf. Deut. 23:3–6; 25:17–19).

Second, how can the expression "enemy" be understood, and to whom should it be applied? If one takes into account the specific examples that follow—"your persecutors" (v. 44b), "those who love you" (v. 46), "your brother" (v. 47)—we must conclude that the enemies are those who do not love us, who are not our family, who persecute us. They are the strangers to Judaism (and the Christian community), the enemies of religion, but also all those who hate us and wish us evil.

It is to these that one must extend universal love and kindness, "so that you may be sons of your Father who is in heaven; for he makes his sun rise on the evil and on the good, and sends rain on the just and the unjust" (v. 45, RSV). This love will manifest itself in prayer for the persecutors (v. 44b), gestures of kindness (v. 46), and friendly relations (greetings, v. 47). By loving one's enemies one becomes like God and not like the publicans and pagans who are kind only to their friends.

Luke's version (6:27–28, 32–36), though substantially the same, does not contain the antithesis but adds other concrete actions to Matthew's list: do good to one's enemies (vv. 27, 33) and bless them (v. 28). Added to these and indicative of Luke's thinking is a recommendation that is more a factor of gratuitous kindness than love of enemies: "lending without any hope of return" (vv. 34–35), as in Matthew 5:42b.

Matthew's last antithesis, and the entire collection, is concluded with the solemn exhortation: "You must therefore be perfect just as your heavenly Father is perfect" (v. 48).

Living according to the demands of these antitheses makes the disciple a whole person, lacking nothing: he or she is *teleios*, "perfect" (see p. 65). Luke, more sensitive to the dimension of gratuitous kindness, expresses this concept differently in the parallel text (Luke 6:36): "Be compassionate as your Father is compassionate."

7. CONCLUSION

The six antitheses that we have just examined are very important because of their content, but also because in them Jesus' sovereign authority is affirmed. Indeed, in certain cases there is not only a transcending or deepening of the Law, but a suppression of the Law (i.e., divorce, oath-taking). Such a stance assumes an awareness on Jesus' part that in his very being and mission he could contradict even the law of God.

Thus the most critical exegetes[13] agree that the roots of such opposition to—radicalization of—the Law can be traced to Jesus. If Matthew was able to construct some antitheses (almost certainly the one on divorce), he must have received most of the others from a preexisting tradition. Three of these antitheses (anger, evil desire, oath-taking) have no parallel elsewhere; two find corresponding sections in Luke (vengeance, love of enemies); the one on divorce is encountered elsewhere in the Synoptics.

The demands these antitheses present are fundamentally oriented toward one's neighbor, as is immediately evident from the first (anger), and from the fifth and the sixth (vengeance, love of enemies). Disciples must love their neighbor, their sister or brother, avoiding inner or outer dispositions that might destroy their fraternal rapport. But even more, they are called to an almost impossible task. They are not to resist their aggressor or the one who seeks to do them harm. Rather, they must yield and even do more than is required. In addition, they must not be content with allowing themselves to be forced or victimized, but they must positively love the enemy who persecutes them and concretely manifest kindness toward that enemy.

Two other antitheses (divorce, oath-taking) ultimately have the same orientation. In the case of the prohibition on divorce, one must trust the other and not break the immediate bond with that person or the larger bonds of human justice and fidelity. The exclusion of all oath-taking and the call for true honesty assume that human relationships should be transparent, that word and thought should coincide, that there should be no need of intermediaries, even divine ones, to confirm them.

What remains are the antitheses that correlate desire and action. At first glance they seem to address only inner life, the source of choices and actions and the criteria of an individual's values. The example given is oriented toward the sexual and hence the relational dimension. Even before it finds expression, the inner desire has already manipulated another and perhaps wounded that other one (adultery).

These antitheses, like the Beatitudes and the texts that follow, demonstrate that the realm of human relationships is called to a radical transformation. In deference to their neighbor, Christians must transcend themselves, their defenses, and the self-centered affirmation of their rights.

The recipients of the message are those who wish to practice the justice Jesus taught; there is no other way. If one can speak about the radicalism of celibacy (see pp. 56 ff.), one must do as much for conjugal fidelity. The refusal of divorce, presented as an antithesis of the Law, demonstrates that the Christian community and the evangelist thought that such behavior was as demanding and difficult as nonresistance and love of enemies.

Motivating participation in such justice is the call and the authority of Jesus. He alone can widen, deepen, and even reverse the framework of the Law to extend it further. Such unusual behavior is proposed only by virtue of Jesus' declaration, "but, I say to you." It was not the formula (customary among the rabbis) but the unparalleled content of the demand that surprised his listeners.

With this authority Jesus reveals the all-encompassing justice one must embrace in order to enter into the kingdom of heaven. But the deepest motivation, which should inspire and make possible such conduct, is the motivation to be like God, like the heavenly Father. Matthew says "be perfect" as the Father is perfect. Luke, no doubt more faithful to the original meaning, says "be compassionate." In fact, the summary demand that these antitheses make of the disciples is to practice a kindness so gratuitous, unconditional, efficacious, and tender that the only possible model is the mercy (*oiktirmon/oiktirmoi* designates "the bowels") of the one whose compassion for men and women is renewed each morning (Lam. 3:22–23).

DO NOT JUDGE BUT FORGIVE

Among the six antitheses in the Sermon on the Mount (Matt. 5:21–48), three were directly concerned with the neighbor (avoid anger, do not resist the evil one, love your enemies); the last two have Lucan parallels.

After a collection of various tests—good works done in secret (Matt. 6:1–18), teachings to the rich and the poor (Matt. 6:19–34; see pp. 77–83)—Matthew returns to the theme of neighbor (Matt. 7:1–5). The Lucan parallel (Luke 6:37–42), by immediately following a teaching on loving one's enemies (6:27–36) with its concluding exhortation to "Be compassionate as your Father is compassionate" (6:36), clearly establishes the connection between the two themes.

1. DO NOT JUDGE (MATT. 7:1-2)

Matthew's text contains two verses on judgment (Matt. 7:1-2) and is followed by the apologue on the splinter and the plank (7:3-5). Luke's text is a little longer and contains more disparate themes: "If you want to avoid judgment, stop passing judgment. Your verdict on others will be the verdict passed on you. The measure with which you measure will be used to measure you" (Matt. 7:1, NAB).

The concept of not passing judgment is made more explicit by Luke: "Do not judge, and you will not be judged yourselves; do not condemn, and you will not be condemned yourselves; grant pardon and you will be pardoned [*apoluete*]" (Luke 6:37). Luke follows this text with an exhortation on gratuitous giving in which he uses the image of measuring (see pp. 90-92).

In this saying Jesus excludes all forms of judgment or condemnation of one's neighbor. One cannot know the inner workings of another's heart. Even if one observes others' apparent misconduct, ultimately the motives and the responsibility for it are beyond that observing person's grasp. One must always be more inclined to kindness, mercy, and forgiveness if one wants the divine judgment one faces on the last day to have the same characteristics. Thus these few words suggest that there is a wide gulf; it is never possible to make a true and decisive judgment on one's neighbor. The final word is God's alone—and I must hope he will be merciful to me then as I try now to be merciful to my brothers and sisters.

A second consideration raises a deep psychological question. Rather than consider the faults, the erring ways of my neighbor, why not first of all consider my own, which are much greater? The apologue of the splinter and the plank is related in almost identical terms by Matthew/Luke (Matt. 7:3-5):

3 Why do you observe the splinter in your brother's eye and never notice the plank in your own?

4 How dare you say to your brother, "Let me take the splinter out of your eye," when all the time there is a plank in your own?

5 Hypocrite! Take the plank out of your own eye first, and

then you will see clearly enough to take the splinter out of your brother's eye.

Even more than the excluding of all judgment, this apologue encourages leniency and tolerance of one's neighbor's faults, motivated by an awareness of one's own wretchedness.

2. FORGIVE (MATT. 6:14-15)

We encountered in Luke 6:37 the expression *apoluô*, which can be translated "discharge," "dismiss," "acquit." Nonresistance of the evil one, the love of enemies, and the exclusion of judgment are possible and have meaning only if accompanied by acquittal, by forgiveness. Not to judge or condemn when one sees evil in others and this evil wounds us is to open for the neighbor a door out of the present evil into a future with infinite possibilities of reconciliation and love.

Just at the moment when Jesus is giving the "Our Father" to his disciples (6:9-13), Matthew inserts the teaching on forgiveness:

14 For if you forgive others the wrongs they have done, your heavenly Father will also forgive you;

15 but if you do not forgive others, then the wrongs you have done will not be forgiven by your Father. [NEB]

The equivalent of verse 14 can be found in Mark (11:25), perhaps in its original context: before every prayer, one must have forgiven one's neighbor, so as to stand reconciled before God. Such is likewise the meaning of the parable on liturgical offering and reconciliation (Matt. 5:23-24); the latter prevails over the former (see pp. 108-9). Thus the mention of forgiveness, common to Matthew/Luke, is associated with the idea of prayer and God's forgiveness. The condition for being forgiven by God is the prior forgiveness granted to one's neighbor.

Another text on forgiveness (Matthew/Luke) considers its frequency. Matthew places it in the discourse on the church (chap. 18). In Luke (17:3-4) it is presented as a simple logion without any such setting:

3b If your brother sins, rebuke him, and if he repents, forgive him;

4 and if he sins against you seven times in the day, and turns to you seven times, and says, "I repent," you must forgive him. [RSV]

The first part of the logion (v. 3b) has a much more developed parallel in Matthew where it becomes a three-stage process of fraternal correction (Matt. 18:15–17). The second part (v. 4) appears in Matthew as a dialogue (18:21–22):

21 Then Peter went up to him and said, "Lord, how often must I forgive my brother if he wrongs me? As often as seven times?"

22 Jesus answered, "Not seven, I tell you, but seventy-seven times."

One will notice that in Luke the pardon presupposes the repentance of the offender; in Matthew, however, forgiveness is unconditional. The Matthean presentation in dialogue form as well as going "above and beyond" to forgive (seventy-seven times) could be a creation of the evangelist. Unconditional and unlimited forgiveness is an inexhaustible demand. The word "brother" implies one in close proximity, and since no mention is made of family, it is members of the faith community (both Jewish and Christian) who are challenged here. In daily relationships occasions for clashes, wrongs, and hurting present themselves; only constantly renewed forgiveness can hold the community together. Elsewhere Luke presents us with the supreme model of forgiveness when he has the crucified Jesus say, "Father, forgive them; they do not know what they are doing" (Luke 23:34).

3. CONCLUSION

The two passages on judgment and forgiveness assume the presence of evil in interpersonal relationships and propose the means to conquer it. By leaving ultimate judgment to God, by abstaining from all condemnation, by continually opening the door to reconciliation, the disciple keeps love and communion alive. When one is familiar with how selfish, hardhearted, and cruel men and women can be, one sees how extraordinary this demand is. To judge not and to forgive continually express what is most radical about love—namely, victory over acknowledged and confronted evil.

The disciple is committed to this way because the evil he or she would be inclined to denounce and condemn is found, first of all, within (the splinter and the plank). The way we behave towards our neighbor is the very same way God will behave toward us, with judgment as well as forgiveness.

GOOD WORKS DONE IN SECRET (MATT. 6:1-18)

The justice of believers and their way of life as disciples of Jesus must flourish vigorously (Matt. 5:20, RSV). It must extend further than the Law, transcend it, even occasionally oppose it. Such is the meaning of the antitheses (Matt. 5:21-48), placed precisely after the declaration that the disciples' justice must exceed that of the Pharisees. The disciples' conduct, by its fullness and oddness, astonishes others and stands out before them like "salt" and "light" (Matt. 5:13-14); it must nonetheless be different from that of the hypocrites (Matt. 6:2, 5, 16): "Be careful not to parade your good deeds before men to attract their notice; by doing this you will lose all reward from your Father in heaven" (Matt. 6:1).

After this inscription from his own hand, Matthew shows how to avoid performing acts of almsgiving (6:2-4), prayer (6:5-6), and fasting (6:16-18)—three major observances of Jewish piety (Tob. 12:8)—before others but, rather, to wait for a reward from God alone.

These three examples, perfectly constructed in an identical schema, are not creations of the evangelist. They contain all the traits of Jesus' authentic teachings.[14] In contrast to these religious practices, already denounced in Judaism[15] as well as by Jesus (Matt. 23:13-15), Matthew proposes detachment, discretion, and doing good works in secret.

1. ALMSGIVING (MATT. 6:2-4)

2 So when you give alms [or exercise mercy], do not have it trumpeted before you; this is what the hypocrites do in

the synagogues and in the streets to win men's admiration. I tell you solemnly, they have their reward.

3 But when you give alms, your left hand must not know what your right is doing;

4 your almsgiving must be secret, and your Father who sees all that is done in secret will reward you.

This small masterpiece of observation and irony invites the disciples to avoid ostentation and vain glory. If one "must give to the poor" (and God only knows how often this saying was repeated by Jesus), it is not to appear generous and virtuous in the eyes of others or to receive their congratulations. One should not even be too aware of what one is doing and not take oneself too seriously ("your left hand must not know what your right is doing"). Generosity, simplicity of heart, humility about one's deeds, avoidance of pious exhibitionism—this is what Jesus proposes. Surrounded in secrecy, the gift does not humiliate the poor or make the donor proud, but is seen and observed by the Father. And the reward, the true one, will be given by God alone.

We must note the apparent paradox in this text. On the one hand, Jesus' disciples are invited to act in secret, unseen by others, and without expecting any praise from them; even more, the disciple must not dwell on his or her good deed. On the other hand, a reward is promised from the Father who sees what is done in secret. The passage does not say that the disciple should act for the sake of a reward—even if it be from God. It merely affirms that an act unknown by men and women is known by God, who will give (in the future) a repayment, a reward. The text does not specify what this reward is or when it will be given. As expressed elsewhere (for example, the judgment episode, Matt. 25:34ff.), the reward is part of the future participation in the life and reign of God, ushered in by Jesus.

2. PRAYER AND FASTING (MATT. 6:5-18)

The same teaching on secrecy covers two other examples: prayer and fasting. We shall quickly examine each, emphasizing only the peculiarities of each pericope:

5 And when you pray, do not imitate the hypocrites: They love to say their prayers standing up in the synagogues

and at the street corners for people to see them. I tell you solemnly, they have had their reward.

6 But when you pray, go to your private room and when you have shut the door, pray to your Father who is in that secret place, and your Father who sees all that is done in secret will reward you.

The action is different (here and in the following pericope, the pronoun "you" is plural, whereas in the almsgiving pericope, the singular "you" was used), but the situation and teaching are identical. Prayer is something that takes place between the individual and God; it is not a show meant to attract the admiration of others.

Matthew then adds three passages, differing in content and form but all related to prayer, which perfectly parallel the passages on almsgiving and fasting. Verses 7 and 8, constructed more or less like the preceding passage, warn against an overabundance of words and their mechanical repetition in prayer. Next, the long version of the prayer of Jesus, the "Our Father," which Matthew (6:9–13) has in common with Luke (Luke 11:2–4), is given. The conclusion develops the theme of forgiveness (vv. 14–15).

The text then broaches the third example, fasting:

16 When you fast, you are not to look glum as the hypocrites do. They change the appearance of their faces so that others may see they are fasting. I assure you they are already repaid.

17 When you fast, see to it that you groom your hair and wash your face.

18 In that way no one can see you are fasting but your Father who is hidden; and your Father who sees what is hidden will repay you. [NAB]

The three examples describe, as we have already noted, three observances of Jewish piety included in Jesus' demands. This is evident for charity (the preceding chapter has abundantly demonstrated this) and for prayer (the "Our Father" is a prayer formula that Jesus left for his disciples). Concerning fasting, even though its regular practice rapidly spread in the Christian milieu (as the Didache in the first century testifies[16]), its basis in the Gospels seems less certain. Our text says nothing on either the obligation or the frequency of fasting; it neither encourages nor discourages fasting. It simply declares that fasting, when practiced (which voices approval, at least) must be done for God and not for others. To know where to stand on the subject of fasting in Jesus' teaching, it is helpful to study a few related texts.

According to Luke, John the Baptist abstained from all alcoholic beverages (Luke 1:15), as a Nazirite would. Matthew/Mark present him eating grasshoppers and wild honey in the desert. Jesus described him as "neither eating nor drinking (Matt. 11:18). Luke specifies "not eating bread, not drinking wine" (Luke 7:33). Certainly these are the traits of one consecrated, a prophetic gesture rather than an ascetical performance. It is said elsewhere, moreover, that John's disciples practiced special fasts like the Pharisees (Mark 2:18). This was a custom observed by pious Jews, as Luke notes in the case of the prophetess Anna (Luke 2:37).

Jesus began his ministry by a sojourn in the desert (Matt. 1:12–13). Matthew and Luke note that he ate nothing for forty days and forty nights (Matt. 4:2). Matthew even uses the specific expression "he fasted." One will notice the same link with the forty-day fasts of Moses (Exod. 34:28) and Elijah (1 Kings 19:8). Neither Jesus nor his disciples, however, practiced any special fasts. Contrary to John the Baptist, Jesus eats and drinks, is a "friend of tax collectors and sinners" (Matt. 11:19), sits at table with them (Matt. 9:10–11; Luke 19:7); he is even accused of being a "glutton and a drunkard" (Matt. 11:19). In the descriptions of the happiness to come, the images of a meal are preferential: the elect will sit at table with Abraham and the faithful of old (Matt. 8:11) and will eat (Luke 14:15) and drink the new wine (Luke 22:18).

Fasting being a sign of mourning, Jesus' disciples are told not to fast while the "bridegroom" is with them (Mark 2:19). The following explanation, "But the time will come for the bridegroom to be taken away from them, and then, on that day, they will fast" (v. 20), was no doubt added to justify the fasting of Christians on Fridays after the death of Christ.[17]

The only other place where Jesus speaks about fasting is the previously analyzed passage on fasting in secret, without outer displays (Matt. 6:16–17).[18] Apart from a few other references to fasting in the New Testament—warnings against excesses in food and drink (Matt. 24:38; Luke 21:34), fasts in preparation for "ordination" (Acts 13:2; 14:23), Paul's fasts (by choice or necessity?; 2 Cor. 6:5; 11:27)—we must acknowledge that this practice receives no special emphasis in Jesus' teaching or in the experience of the primitive community. At any rate, it cannot be put on the same level as the other demands of Jesus: renouncing one's family, sharing one's possessions, celibacy, or the permanency of marriage. Ascetic food practices do not seem to be part of the "radicalism" proposed by the Gospels.

3. CONCLUSION

The same demand emerges from these three examples. When doing good deeds—even those most basic to one's identity as a believer, such as sharing with the poor and praying—the disciple must renounce all ostentation and vanity. Neither discretion, secrecy, nor anonymity are, however, the last word. The disciple must avoid even self-satisfaction, acting as if he or she were unaware of those very deeds. What is required of the disciple is absolute detachment. One must not seek a reward from others or even from one's own good conscience. Only the Father who sees in secret can give the reward.

To whom are these three warnings addressed? Jesus' own preaching is addressed to all hearers, to disciples in the widest possible meaning of the term. Jesus condemned all poor imitations and poor attempts to dupe pious people, which the "hypocrites" were guilty of doing. In the communities for which Matthew writes, all Christians are thus warned; they must not "make appearances" but act in truth and with detachment.

The motivation for such unusual behavior is, as we have noticed, quite paradoxical. One must avoid ostentation which, while evoking praise and congratulations, already constitutes its own reward—a reward that is ultimately empty. Instead one must act in secret, because there is another reward (not described here) that is hidden with God, who knows all secrets. The good deed is not to be done with this reward in mind but, unseen by others, and almost unseen even by the doer, it will be noted by God and rewarded accordingly.

Beyond their apparent complexity, these three passages touch a sensitive point of religious behavior. Jesus' disciples must attain, even in virtuous deeds, a level of extreme detachment. They must not seek either the approval of others or their own self-satisfaction, not even, directly, divine reward. They must perform the deed in all its purity, delegating the judgment and the reward to God.

GENERAL CONCLUSION

In the preceding chapters, the demands focused on severing one's ties with one's trade and family and on accepting itinerancy, insecurity, denying oneself, risking one's life, renouncing possessions, and sharing. The tone of chapter 6 is completely different. In fact, the strongest demands of the Sermon on the Mount, which chapter 6 analyzes (excluding the passages on material possessions), address one's attitude toward God and one's neighbor.

Jesus' disciples must be so intent on the new justice that they will indeed hunger and thirst for it, letting the desire for it fill their hearts, and groan while waiting for its fulfillment. If, because of this, they are persecuted, they will consider themselves blessed (the Beatitudes). But in awaiting the fulfillment of this justice they must not seek to satisfy their own claims, leaving to God alone the right to give rewards (good deeds done in secret).

The essence of this justice can be summed up in the love of neighbor—the Golden Rule, which Matthew/Luke explicitly affirm: "So always treat others as you would like them to treat you; that is the meaning of the Law and the Prophets" (Matt. 7:12).

But this love is presented in its somber aspect. Indeed, what slowly unfolds is not an easy, radiant love but a crucified love. One must love, receive, bear others patiently, even through difficulties and hostilities. If this neighbor provokes me to anger or arouses in me the desire for resistance or revenge so that he becomes my enemy (antitheses), it is precisely this neighbor whom I must abstain from judging and condemning. I must forgive, show mercy to that person, bringing peace and reconciliation. All this requires an inner honesty, a poor and gentle heart.

Thus in the area of relationships, the less visible, inner demands are no less radical. Jesus' new law, which Matthew reveals in his great discourse, reaches the innermost parts of the heart and calls for a letting go of self, a stepping aside. Love here is not desire but reception of the other in all his or her otherness, even when negative or hostile. Matthew perceives how difficult this is, and at the end of the discourse he includes Jesus' sayings on the two gates and the two ways (Matt. 7:13–14). The gate that opens into life and the road that leads to it are narrow, and few take the risk; but the gate and road of perdition are wide and often taken. To live the demands of merciful love requires an effort of which few are capable. Luke's parallel version (13:23–24), though in a different context (the number of the elect), is more insistent: "strive to enter by the narrow gate" (RSV).

On the redactional level there is no doubt that the totality of this discourse is addressed to all of Jesus' hearers and, beyond them, to all those who receive the gospel. To the extent that one can trace elements to their precommunal level, they do not seem to be destined to any particular group but are addressed to all the various strata of the Jewish world and are in contrast with their practices. The radicalism of love upheld by this discourse is required of all those who want their justice to surpass that of the scribes and the Pharisees in order to enter into the kingdom of heaven (Matt. 5:20).

Such conduct presupposes various motives. Those who practice this radical love are already—and will be absolutely in the future—blessed and the kingdom belongs to them. They will be like their Father in heaven, merciful and perfect. Such is the reward promised to them and which will be given to them by the Father who sees in secret. Forgiveness and abstention from judgment are also required because of the weakness and the sin of both parties, but also because they constitute the measure by which God will measure us.

NOTES

1. Dupont, *Les Béatitudes*, Études Bibliques (Paris: Gabalda, 1969), 3:429.

2. Ibid., 3:470.

3. Ibid., 3:603.

4. Ibid., 3:545.

5. Ibid., 3:637.

6. Ibid., 3:457.

7. A good summary of the question can be found in Boismard, *Synopse de quatre évangiles en français*, 2 vols. (Paris: Cerf, 1972), 2:138–39.

8. The unique character of such an interdict is clearly emphasized by Braun, *Spätjüdisch—häretischer und früchristlicher Radikalismus,* 2 vols. (Tübingen: J. C. B. Mohr, 1969), 2:89, n. 3; 2:108–14. Braun thinks that the saying can probably be traced back to Jesus: ibid., 2:110, n. 1.

9. On the meaning of the "Matthean clause," see Matura, "Le célibat dans le Nouveau Testament d'après l'exégèse récente," *Nouvelle Revue Théologique* 97 (1975): 495.

10. Braun, *Spätjüdisch,* 2:80–83.

11. Ibid., 2:57–61.

12. Boismard, *Synopse,* 2:150.

13. This is Braun's thesis in his oft-quoted work, *Spätjüdisch.*

14. Bultmann, *Die Geschichte der synoptischen Tradition* (Göttingen: Vanderhoeck and Ruprecht, 1967), p. 156; Minear, *Commands of Christ,* (Nashville: Abingdon, 1972), pp. 66–68.

15. For rabbinic quotations from the first century tending in this direction, see Manson, *The Sayings of Jesus* (London: SCM Press, 1971), p. 164.

16. According to the Didache (8:1), Christians fasted on Wednesdays and Fridays; J. P. Audet, *La Didache,* Études Bibliques (Paris: Gabalda, 1958).

17. Boismard, *Synopse,* 2:115.

18. In Mark 9:28, "this kind [of demon] can only be driven out by prayer [and fasting]," the word "fasting" is almost universally considered as a nonauthentic addition.

7

Independent Sayings

The texts examined in the four preceding chapters all revolved around a common theme: the call to discipleship and its demands (chap. 3); renunciation (chap. 4); the use and sharing of possessions (chap. 5); the radicalization of the Law, especially its demands toward one's neighbor (chap. 6). A certain number of Jesus' sayings—we have retained nine—are not contained in any of these groupings but are nonetheless connected with radicalism.

Most of these sayings are found as independent logia, not being part of any particular collection. Only one, "the last will be first" is common to all three Synoptic Gospels (Mark 10:31). Four belong to the double tradition: "not peace, but the sword" (Matt. 10:34-36); "the kingdom subjected to violence" (Matt. 11:12); "the narrow gate" (Matt. 7:13-14); "he who is not with me is against me" (Matt. 12:30). One is reported by Mark/Matthew: the hand or foot that causes one to sin (Mark 9:43-45). Two are peculiar to Luke: count the cost before commitment (Luke 14:28-32); the useless servants (Luke 17:7-10). One is retained only by Matthew: "many are called, but few are chosen" (Matt. 22:14).

What binds together these apparently disparate sayings—and the reason for studying them in the same chapter—is that they all insist on the rigors of the task, caution one to consider what is at stake, and give images that show the risk and the cost of the undertaking.

Three of these sayings have already been mentioned in the

course of the preceding analyses: not peace but the sword (see pp. 34–35); count the cost (see p. 54); and the narrow gate (see p. 126). We shall, however, approach them from a different angle: the difficulty of living radically.

WORDS OF ENCOURAGEMENT:
THE LAST WILL BE FIRST (MARK 10:31)

This paradox indicating the reversal of a situation appears four times in the Synoptics—twice in Matthew, concluding the pericope on rewards (Matt. 19:27–30) and the parable of the workers in the vineyard (Matt. 20:16); once in Mark (10:31), in the same context as Matthew 19:30; once in Luke, concluding a passage on the small number of those who will be saved (13:30).

We see that the context is not always the same. In fact, there are three very different ones. The most immediately comprehensible context is found in Luke. The passage describes salvation or entrance into the kingdom of God (Luke 13:23–30). To the general question, "will there be only a few saved?" (v. 23), Jesus responds with three successive images: the narrow gate into salvation; the great effort needed to enter; the many who will fail (v. 24). Moreover, at a given moment the gate will be closed, and no matter what the appeal the master will not open it, even to those who claim to have eaten and drunk with him or heard him preach on their streets (vv. 25–27: alluding to the Jews). They will be thrust away from him, from the patriarchs and prophets assembled in the kingdom (v. 28). People coming from all points on the compass will take their seats at the feast (v. 29). This is when the logion appears, and its meaning is very clear: "Yes, there are those now last who will be first, and those now first who will be last."

Jesus responds to the question of the number of Jews who will be saved by making the observation that very few of them will commit themselves to his way. Thus they risk being excluded from the messianic feast, while many "pagans" will gain access to it. Thus the "last," strangers, latecomers will be the first to enter the kingdom, while Jews, who should rightfully have priority, will be the last. The logion addresses a historical situation that Jesus found deplorable and wanted his people to avoid.

The same saying is found in a very different context in Mark/ Matthew (Mark 10:31). It occurs after the pericope where Jesus promises that the disciples who have left all for him will receive "a hundred times over . . . and . . . eternal life" (Mark 10:28–30). We must admit that this expression does not make much sense directly following this passage. Who are the last and first in this context? Referring to the two preceding passages does not clarify the dilemma: the rich young man (Mark 10:17–22); the difficulty for the rich to be saved (Mark 10:23–27).

We are obliged to assume, as have some exegetes,[1] that, as we have already said, Mark's narrative on the danger of riches is a composite text (see p. 69). The first part (vv. 23, 25) considers riches as an obstacle to salvation; the second, more absolute (vv. 24, 26–27), affirms the general difficulty of salvation and parallels Luke's narrative mentioned above (Luke 13:23–30). Mark's verse 31 initially may have served as the conclusion of a collection on the difficulty (for the Jews) of being saved, similar to Luke's context. Modifications and additions may have left it as the ending of the collection on the rich young man, the difficulty of riches, and the promised reward. Its initial meaning, obviously lost in the present context, would have been the same as the Lucan pericope analyzed above (13:23–30).

Matthew uses the maxim to conclude the parable of the vineyard workers (20:16). Those who come last, those who have worked less, are the first to receive the same salary as the workers of the early hour. The latecomers are favored, thus reversing the normal roles and priorities. They may be (and it is most likely) the "sinners" whom Jesus calls to conversion and who, having arrived last, have the right to receive mercy (the salary) first. Or again, they may be pagans and Jews (as previously in Luke). In either case, Matthew's application of the maxim retains its initial meaning.

What conclusion can be drawn regarding the relationship of this saying to the theme of radicalism? I think that more than the indication of a demand, we find beatitudes (in Luke's version), divine promises. God's kindness reaches first and foremost the "poor," the despised, those rejected by the religious and secular world. The last, the pagans (Luke 13:29), the publicans, and the prostitutes (Matt. 21:31) will precede into God's kingdom those who think they have first rights to it (Matt. 21:32). This saying introduces a difficult discourse on what is at stake in decision-making while constituting an invitation and an encouragement for the poor.

THE INELUCTABLE CHOICE: "HE WHO IS NOT WITH ME IS AGAINST ME" (MATT. 12:30)

In Matthew/Luke this logion concludes the narrative about Jesus being accused of chasing away demons in the name of Beelzebul (Matt. 12:22–30). The Pharisees insinuate that he performs miracles with the help of the prince of demons; Jesus responds with three arguments: (1) could Satan be in opposition to himself? (vv. 25–26); (2) it is by the Spirit (or the hand) of God that one chases devils away (vv. 27–28); (3) he is stronger than Satan (v. 29). Then comes verse 30: "He who is not with me is against me, and he who does not gather with me scatters."

The link of this declaration with the preceding episode is not immediately evident. Taken by itself, it indicates that, when the kingdom of God has come in Jesus and manifests itself by the expulsion of demons, his fiercest adversaries, neutrality is no longer possible. One must choose to keep one's distance or not. Seeking other explanations is not neutrality but an opposing choice. The one who is not committed for Jesus is in fact against him.

Another logion (Mark 9:40 and Luke 9:50) specifies what is meant by "not being with." John, the son of Zebedee, who is upset because a man not belonging to the group of disciples is chasing demons away in the name of Jesus (Mark 9:38–41), is cautioned (Luke 9:50): "You must not stop him: anyone who is not against you is for you."

If, then, neutrality is not possible and choosing is unavoidable, the latter can in some way be implicit. Even if one is not formally with Jesus (following in his footsteps, Mark 9:38; Luke 9:49), the fact of invoking his name presupposes that a profound choice has already been made and that one is not against but for Jesus.

Thus this logion (even though a nuance of difference exists in Luke's version) excludes any suspension of choice. When the situation is Jesus and the kingdom bursting forth in the world, choosing is not optional. Furthermore, not to be *for* means being against. In this case, the radicalism makes the choice an urgent one.

THE STAKES AND THE COST

Under this heading, we shall regroup and examine seven other sayings that describe what it costs to accept the demands of Jesus.

1. "NOT . . . PEACE, BUT A SWORD" (MATT. 10:34–36)

34 Do not suppose that I have come to bring peace to the earth; it is not peace I have come to bring, but a sword.

This strange saying, as cited here from Matthew's text, is reported by the double tradition (Luke 12:51). Luke gives it a slightly different form by removing the sword image: "Do you suppose that I am here to bring peace on earth? No, I tell you, but rather division."

In both cases, the logion is followed by a text inspired by Micah (7:6) and which specifies the meaning. The sword, that is to say division, will cut through to the very heart of the most protected of relationships—the family: the son and the father, the daughter and the mother, the daughter-in-law and the mother-in-law.

Matthew also places this declaration close to the missionary discourse (chap. 10). After enumerating those being sent out (10:1–4) and giving them instructions (10:5–16), Jesus warns of persecution (10:17–25; see pp. 34–36) and exhorts them to be courageous in their proclamation (10:26–33). Our logion is placed next (10:34–36), followed by sayings on renunciation (10:37–39; see pp. 52–56). We see here how Matthew has assembled in one single collection various teachings of Jesus on the difficulties, persecutions, and divisions that the disciples sent out on mission can expect.

Luke's collection is not so extensive as Matthew's. The saying relates only to the two verses immediately preceding, where Jesus speaks of the "fire" that he desires to kindle upon earth and the baptism that he must receive (Luke 12:40–50). He is referring to the Passion he must undergo (baptism as suffering: see Mark 10:39), and, likely, the sending forth of the Spirit.[2]

Let us return to the text itself and its relationship to our general theme. The coming of Jesus and the impact of his message, instead of creating unity and peace, provoke heartrending conflicts and division. The disciples (for Matthew, the twelve; for Luke, all disciples) must expect this situation; they know that Jesus' words are not a sedative but a fire. If they are seriously committed to following Jesus they will encounter opposition—all the more painful because it comes from the family, the most vital and intimate setting of one's life. But the disciple is forewarned of what is at stake in this choice. It must be noted that these sayings of Jesus (especially in Luke's context) portray anguish and suffering (fire and baptism). The one who proclaims the love of God and of others will begin by causing division and ruptures.

2. "THE VIOLENT TAKE IT BY FORCE" (MATT. 11:12)

This saying of Jesus, recorded by the double tradition (Matt. 11:12; Luke 16:16), is one of the more difficult texts of the Gospels. Exegetes have found as many as six possible meanings for it.[3] This text, moreover, takes on two considerably different forms. In Matthew it reads as follows:

> 12 From John the Baptizer's time until now the kingdom of God has suffered violence [or has been coming violently, *biazetai*], and the violent take it by force. [NAB]

Luke's text is shorter (16:16): "Up to the time of John it was the Law and the Prophets: Since then, the kingdom of God has been preached, and by violence [*biazetai*] everyone is getting in."

The difficulty arises initially from the words *biazetai* and *biastès*, which are encountered only here.[4] In addition, the context does not allow us to decide whether Jesus is making a sad observation and laying blame or whether he is expressing praise or encouragement.

The interpreters are divided along two main lines. Are the "violent" the adversaries of Jesus (Pharisees) or political rebels (Zealots), who would want to make the kingdom of God (as they conceive it) happen through violence? Sadly Jesus observes this and condemns both the violent and the violence. In the case of approbation, he would be praising violence and encouraging the violent to seize the kingdom. We would also need to know what kind of violence is involved in both cases. Is it the same?

Finally, the third question is whether the two evangelists give the same meaning to the logion, Luke's obviously being the easiest to define. Because we cannot here enter into a detailed, complex exegesis, let us simply present the interpretation that seems most solid and most related to radicalism.[5] As we pointed out earlier, Luke's version is relatively easy to understand. He presents an independent saying outside of any context. For him, until the coming of John the Baptist the Law and the prophets (the old covenant) held sway. John represents a turning point, the passage to a new system, for it is from that point on that the kingdom of God is proclaimed (by Jesus) and that "by violence [biazetai] everyone is getting in." Matthew's text basically carries the same meaning. The word biazetai, translated in Luke as "by violence everyone is getting in," should be similarly translated in Matthew. We would then have this text: the kingdom of God exercises (its) violence, imposes itself forcefully, from the fact that it is proclaimed by Jesus, and it is through great effort that the "violent" seize it. This violence, this great effort are the radical demands of Jesus, which Matthew reports elsewhere: to cut off what causes one to sin (Matt. 5:29–30); not to serve two masters (6:24); to renounce one's family and accept death (10:37–39).

Taken in this way, the saying is obviously related to the theme of radicalism. The kingdom of God, in spite of appearances, irresistably makes its way with power (Mark 9:2 speaks of the kingdom of God "coming with power"). To this overwhelming movement of the kingdom should correspond a parallel undertaking by the disciple. Neither the nature of this undertaking nor the concrete deeds are specified. But the events will be "violent," requiring an extraordinary effort, similar to the effort needed to seize a prey (harpazo) or assault a fortress. The reception of the kingdom is not simply a passive one; it requires the highest effort. Only the violent, ready for anything, everything, who do not slacken their desire will be able to seize it. The kingdom is given only at this cost.

3. "IF YOUR HAND IS YOUR UNDOING . . ." (MARK 9:43–47)

The violence residing within the disciple and the effort needed to seize the kingdom are brutally spotlighted in a logion of Jesus which says that one may have to sacrifice, if need be, the very parts of one's body:

43 If your hand is your undoing [*skandalisè*] cut it off; it is better for you to enter life maimed than to keep both hands and go to hell and the unquenchable fire.
44 [repeats v. 48; omitted by most MSS]
45 And if your foot is your undoing cut it off; it is better to enter into life a cripple than to keep both your feet and be thrown into hell.
46 [repeats v. 48; omitted by most MSS]
47 And if it is your eye, tear it out; it is better to enter into the kingdom of God with one eye than to keep both eyes and be thrown into hell
48 where the devouring worm never dies and their fire is not quenched. [NEB]

In Mark this text is part of a collection of instructions related to scandalizing: one must not scandalize the little ones—better to be "thrown into the sea with a great millstone" around one's neck (Mark 9:42)! This text is reported twice by Matthew, once in a somewhat extended but similar context, and again in an abridged form in the Sermon on the Mount (concerning secret desires and adultery, Matt. 5:27). It suffices here simply to indicate the major modifications.

First, Matthew places the hand and the foot in the same sentence. Second, he mentions only the eye and the hand (reversing Mark's order: hand, foot, eye). In addition, he indicates the right hand and the right eye. In comparison with Mark's text, Matthew's double examples (eye, hand) seem less primitive and there is an implication of sexual behavior because of the mention of adultery.

The verses that we have quoted have a full meaning by themselves, and their link (Mark/Matt.) with the theme of scandalizing the little ones of the community is perhaps not primitive. Luke also transmits this saying (Luke 17:1-2), with the meaning that the scandal is one's own undoing.

The meaning of the text, as Mark presents it, is relatively clear. When anything becomes an obstacle or a stumbling block for the disciple, it must be diligently and ruthlessly cast aside. To fall and not to arise again signifies exclusion from life and rejection into the fire of Gehenna.

Nothing specifically describes the "scandal" or the "undoing." One must not, then, simply affix a moralistic meaning: "an occasion for sin." It is, no doubt, whatever delays and ultimately prevents believers from accepting the message of Jesus and from making it the center of their lives. One must decide: Should I cast this obstacle aside? The image, that very basic body parts—the hand, the foot, the eye (and even the right hand and eye, Matt. 5:29-30)—must be unhesitatingly sacrificed if the need arises, demonstrates how far one must be willing to go. The stakes are so tremendously high—life itself—that one must accept losing what is most precious, the most important parts of one's body.

We have here one of the typical radical sayings—a specific demand bordering on literalism, yet not to be taken literally. By way of an image (and what an image!) the absolute character of Jesus' message is reiterated: it is a decisive and costly choice.

4. "STRUGGLE TO ENTER BY THE NARROW DOOR" (LUKE 13:23-24)

The preceding logion insisted on the sacrifice to which one must consent in order to enter into life, for in losing oneself, one finds oneself again (cf. Matt. 10:39). The saying on the narrow door, even if it does not directly give a demand, describes a difficult situation. This saying, which we have already briefly discussed (see p. 126), is retained in the double tradition (Matt. 7:13-14). Luke seems to have the most plausible context. When someone asks Jesus, "Are only a few to be saved?" (cf. Luke 13:23a), he responds, "Struggle [*agonizethe*] to get in through the narrow door; for I tell you that many will try to enter and not be able" (NEB).

What follows is a three-stage development: (1) once the gate is closed, even Jesus' companions will not be admitted to the feast in the kingdom (vv. 25–28); (2) many strangers (pagans) will come from every direction to the feast (v. 29); and (3) "the last shall be first" (see pp. 129–31).

This collection in which Luke places the saying on the narrow door helps better to explain its meaning. In Luke the audience is Jewish; the number of those who will be saved is a concern of Jews and not of pagans. Thus the first answer would mean: do not imagine that salvation (as preached by Jesus) will come to you automatically. It is not sufficient to be a child of Abraham (v. 28) and a contemporary of Jesus to be admitted to the messianic feast; one must accept Jesus' message and its demands. To do so is like trying to pass through a narrow door where already a crowd is gathered. One must struggle, elbow one's way by, in order to sneak through. Luke's text describes a crowd pressed around a narrow door. Only the strongest succeed in getting through. This clearly means that without a rigorous effort to receive it, the Jews will be excluded from the messianic salvation. Matthew places this saying toward the end of the Sermon on the Mount (Matt. 7:13–14) and makes several modifications in form and meaning:

13 Enter by the narrow gate, since the road that leads to perdition is wide and spacious, and many take it;
14 but it is a narrow gate and a hard road that leads to life, and only a few find it.

Luke's door becomes a gateway (to the city) in Matthew. The image of the road is added and brought to the forefront. There is an opposition between the gate/narrow road and the gate/spacious road. The narrow road is rarely taken and few go through the gate leading to it, but there is a crowd on the spacious road.

In Matthew this small collection prefaces the concluding part of the sermon, whose principal message is that one must be committed with concrete acts ("you will know them by their fruits": Matt. 7:15–20, RSV) and not merely with words (Matt. 7:21–23).

One must build on rock and not on sand (Matt. 7:24–27). Thus the logion on the narrow gate in Matthew is not a warning addressed to Jews on the necessity and the difficulty of choosing to follow Jesus, but rather, a warning to all readers of the Gospel that the road of justice is difficult, narrow, and rarely taken.

In Luke this logion is a statement about, and especially a challenge to, Jesus' Jewish audience. They are told that they may not rely on their privileged origins (see Luke 3:8), but must commit themselves to the way opened by Jesus. Matthew warns all believers of the difficulties ahead of those who respond to the radical demands given in the Sermon on the Mount.

5. "FOR MANY ARE CALLED, BUT FEW ARE CHOSEN" (MATT. 22:14)

The brief sentence "For many are called, but few are chosen" has no direct parallel in the other Gospels ("the last shall be first" does not have the same meaning). Only Matthew includes it. In his Gospel it concludes the parable of those invited to the royal wedding feast (Matt. 22:1–14); Luke tells a slightly different version (Luke 14:15–24). In this double parable a king is preparing a wedding feast for his son (vv. 2–3). Despite repeated reminders, those invited refuse to come and some even abuse the messengers (vv. 4–6), which angers the king, who punishes the offenders (v. 7). The king then invites those who are passing by in the streets, the good and the bad, and the wedding hall is filled (vv. 8–10). Matthew then adds the parable of the guest without a wedding garment who is expelled from the feast. This is where the verse in question is placed.

The text contains a double teaching. The first parable makes three points through images: the messianic calling; the refusal of those first invited, namely, the Jews; and the massive entrance of pagans into the Christian community. The second parable is addressed to this community with a warning against presumptions. It is not sufficient to be within the wedding hall (the community), but one must have a wedding garment (the works of justice).

The meaning of the parable is clear; the relationship between the final maxim and the two-part parable, however, is more obscure. In the first part, some are called, but none is chosen; in the second part, all those called, except one, are chosen. The maxim probably is a logion of Jesus that initially circulated in an isolated form and, like the parables on the "last" and the "narrow gate," was addressed to the Jews. Matthew probably wanted to connect the warning in this double parable with a universal call to salvation, which nevertheless does not automatically entail a response. Many who are called refuse (everyone in the first parable), and even those who accept are not necessarily allowed to stay (the guest without a proper garment).

When taken alone, outside its context (a superficial one, at that), this well-coined phrase does not say anything different from what we previously examined. The call is generous and universal, but some, instead of accepting it, will oppose it through indifference or refusal. Once again we hear a warning and a challenge: be careful, an effort is required in order to be one of the chosen. The call is only a preliminary step; the response is what counts, and is not to be taken for granted.

6. COUNTING THE COST (LUKE 14:28-32)

While examining the sayings on renunciation reported by the double tradition, we noted that Luke inserted a double parable between the second and third logia (see pp. 54–55).

After having declared that one cannot be a disciple of Jesus without hating one's next of kin as well as one's own life and without carrying one's cross, Luke, instead of immediately moving to the third declaration of the same type ("anyone who does not renounce all his possessions cannot be my disciple"), introduces two brief narratives (chap. 14):

28 For which of you, desiring to build a tower, does not first sit down and count the cost, whether he has enough to complete it?

29 Otherwise, when he has laid a foundation and is not able to finish, all who see it begin to mock him,

30 saying, "This man began to build, and was not able to finish."

31 Or what king, going to encounter another king in war,

will not sit down first and take counsel whether he is able
with ten thousand to meet him who comes against him
with twenty thousand?

32 And if not, while the other is yet a great way off, he
sends an embassy and asks terms of peace. [RSV]

The meaning of these examples is clear. One must reflect before
acting; otherwise, one may fail and be publicly ridiculed. These
are simple counsels of popular wisdom; it is impossible to know
their origins. But the fact that Luke inserted them between extremely rigorous declarations of Jesus confers on them a certain
gravity. What is asked of someone wanting to follow Jesus transcends ordinary human norms. One must think seriously, evalu-
ate all aspects, and count the cost. These counsels are not meant
to turn one away from the undertaking, but above all to make one
realize the difficulty. In Luke's context they say: do not take these
demands lightly. These demands will ask for your all. If you are
ready to give all, then you can make a commitment. But be forewarned of the price you may pay.

7. "USELESS SERVANTS" (LUKE 17:7-10)

This brief passage, peculiar to Luke and without a larger context, is a curious parable of Jesus. Which master would ask his
servant returning from work to join him at table? Would he not
ask of him instead to perform many other services, first prepare
the meal and serve his master and only then also eat? Would not
the master express his thanks? Jesus responds (Luke 17:10): "It is
quite the same with you who hear me. When you have done all
you have been commanded to do, say, 'We are useless servants.
We have done no more than our duty' " [NAB].

The Greek term *achreioi*, translated literally here as "useless"
(sometimes "merely" or "unworthy") servants, is not first of all
an expression of humility, since in the parable the servant was
useful and did serve well. In the context it means, rather, that he
deserves no special reward because of his work.

The disciples of Jesus (and here, if one is to accept the introduction of chap. 17, "disciples" has a restricted meaning), even when
they have done everything, will still not have satisfied the inex-

haustible demands of God. They do not deserve any salary; God owes them nothing. The only right that they have won is to be able to continue serving the Master's needs. In fact, as Paul says in speaking about his service of the gospel, the responsibility entrusted to him "gives me no grounds for boasting. For a necessity is laid upon me" (1 Cor. 9:16–17). One rediscovers here the meaning of the parable of the vineyard workers (only Matt.) 20: 1–16) who are paid, not according to their work but because God is good.

GENERAL CONCLUSION

We have noted the special character of this chapter's various independent sayings. They are not part of characterized collections or related to any theme already treated, nor do they readily appear to have any points in common with each other. In actuality, however, our analysis reveals that a common element does exist. With one exception, these logia all describe a new situation. Before presenting the demands and specifying them, they affirm that the new situation, created by the coming of Jesus' kingdom, is a crisis situation, imposing and forcing a decision.

The sword and division are introduced into the network of human relationships. One cannot henceforth remain indifferent; one must either be for it or against. The kingdom manifests itself with power and imposes its "violence." This kingdom is like a narrow gate and a hard road, which not everyone is able to take. For even if those called are numerous, the chosen are few. Paradoxically, the last have the chance to be counted first, while those who have worked long and hard are "unworthy servants." Thus these nine sayings that we have assembled express an urgent situation and a pressing challenge addressed to believers in a time of crisis.

This situation requires a response; it creates demands. In the parables, these demands appear as part of the description of a situation when they do not constitute the only point of a text (the saying on the hand causing scandal and the necessity of counting the cost). Since the kingdom exercised its violence, the believer must in turn strive with all his or her strength to seize it; he or she must act "violently." If one must cut off one's hand or foot or tear out one's eye to attain it, it is better to do so than to find oneself denied entrance. The price is dear, but the stakes are high: life or perdition.

The recipients of these challenges could at first have been Jesus' Jewish audience (the "last . . . first," the "narrow gate," the "few that are chosen"). But community custom and, at any rate, Matthew's presentation appeal to the hearers of the gospel, the members of the Christian community. Apart from the parable of the useless servants, none of these sayings is restricted to a category of persons or a particular case. Sooner or later every disciple finds himself or herself in a situation where these sayings become true and their demands imperative.

What underlying motivations are associated with the demands proposed here? The two logia—the scandal of the bodily parts, the narrow door and road—present what is at stake: life or perdition (Gehenna). A choice must be made. The other sayings do not explain the situation, nor do they indicate the reasons for making choices. From the moment that Jesus appears and the kingdom is proclaimed, the sword is drawn. The situation itself is decisive and forces one to choose.

NOTES

1. Boismard, *Synopse de quatre évangiles en français*, 2 vols. (Paris: Cerf, 1972), 2:312–13; Minear, *Commands of Christ* (Nashville: Abingdon, 1972), pp. 106–9.

2. Boismard, *Synopse*, 2:285.

3. Bonnard, *L'Évangile selon Saint Matthieu* (Neuchâtel: Delachaux et Niéstlé, 1970), p. 163; J. Schiewiend, "Das Evangelium nach Matthäus," *Das Neue Testment Deutsch: Die drei ersten Evangelien* (Göttingen: Vanderhoeck and Ruprecht, 1971), p. 144.

4. If *biastès* designates a violent person, the verb *biazetai* can mean either to suffer (undergo) violence in the passive tense or to exercise force by means of violence; examples are Luke 24:29; Acts 16:15 with the compound *parabiazetai*.

5. One rediscovers it in Mason, *The Sayings of Jesus* (London: SCM Press, 1971), p. 134.

8

The Radicalism of the Synoptics and Other New Testament Writings

The texts presented and analyzed until now were all derived from the Synoptic tradition. They allowed us to observe the radical demands in Jesus' teachings as presented by the three Gospel redactors. But the Synoptics are only one part of the New Testament. Other writings, including the Gospel of John and the letters attributed to him, the Acts of the Apostles, the collection of Pauline letters, and the letters of Peter and James, also propose norms of conduct in the name of Jesus or as an act of faith in him. Can one find in these texts equivalents or at least a few parallels to the radicalism so clearly presented by Matthew, Mark, and Luke?

We raised this issue at the beginning of our study, promising to address it adequately at the end. We must now discover whether these other New Testament writings contain themes of radicalism similar to that which has preceded. Such a comparison is difficult, and we risk falling into a "concordance mentality." The Synoptics are presented as recounting historical events concerning Jesus and his teachings during the course of his lifetime. The other writings, and even in a sense John's Gospel, are essentially a message on the risen Christ and the consequences of faith in the lives of believers. The concrete repercussions of such faith can be important and even radical, but they will not necessarily coincide with what Jesus, according to the Synoptics, actually demanded of his hearers.

This reservation—and it is a significant one—having been

stated, we shall seek out other New Testament texts which, at least by their content, bring to mind some demands or radical teachings from the Synoptics. In such cases we shall not necessarily find an echo, even a tenuated one, of the historical teaching of Jesus or the communal tradition that is the source of the Synoptic Gospels. Some reminiscences and memories are possible, but the teaching could also be deductions (consequences of the new Christian lifestyle) developing independently from the witness of the Synoptics.

Having thus indicated the limits of our undertaking, we shall try to make a brief summary of four New Testament collections, the Acts of the Apostles, the Pauline corpus, the Johannine writings, and the letters of James and Peter. The point of our study will be, obviously, to compare their radical resonances with the preceding analyses. And since the focus of our study is the Synoptic Gospels, we shall not make an exhaustive analysis here but only a general presentation of each text. The results of this comparison (the presence of certain demands, the absence of others, their relative importance, the perspective peculiar to each group of writings, etc.) will be presented in the conclusion of this chapter.

THE ACTS OF THE APOSTLES

The Gospel of Luke and the Acts of the Apostles are written by the same author and form a whole. It will be interesting to begin our inquiry with the book of Acts. This will allow us to observe how the author sees the radical instructions of Jesus, strongly emphasized in his Gospel, realized in the life and growth of the Christian community from its origins.

1. THE IDEAL OF SHARING (*KOINONIA*)

As we have seen, Luke's Gospel insists on the duty of divesting oneself in a variety of ways of one's possessions and sharing them with others, especially the poor (see pp. 84–97). Describing the life of the first community of believers in Jerusalem, Luke has the opportunity to show, in a concrete (even if very idealized) manner, how such sharing was actualized. The theme of *koinonia* ("communion," "community") is summed up in two texts: Acts 2:43–44; 4:32–34 (expanded by Acts 4:35; 5:1ff.).

The word *koinonia*, which is almost exclusively Pauline (appearing fourteen times in Paul's writings, only once in Acts, and three times in 1 John 1:3, 6, 7), designates for Luke the sharing of material possessions. The first disciples take great care to apply the teachings of the apostles through *koinonia*, breaking bread, and prayer (Acts 2:42). The concrete practice of *koinonia* is detailed in the passages cited above. First of all, there is a general affirmation (2:44): "And all who believed were together and had all things in common" (RSV), which is then summarized (4:32): "no one said that any of the things which he possessed was his own, but they had everything in common" (RSV).

In fact, those who had possessions sold them (Acts 2:45; 4:34) and placed the proceeds at the feet of the apostles (4:35–37; 5:2) to be shared (2:45) or distributed (4:34) according to the needs of each one (2:45; 4:35). It suffices here to recall, among others, the saying of Jesus, "Go, sell what you have, give it to the poor," to sense that the same theme and the same words are present here.

It is all the more striking to see the differences. The poor here are the members of the community who are in need before the well-off divest themselves, but are not in need after that takes place. What motivates the gesture of sharing is the desire to eliminate poverty and establish equality of all. Thus paradoxically, divestiture of one's possessions does not lead to poverty but to community, fulfilling the command in Deuteronomy, "Let there be no poor among you" (15:4).

We must, however, add that this scene is somewhat undermined by two facts. If the sharing was as widespread as the text seems to affirm, why did Luke feel the need to spotlight the example of Barnabas (Acts 4:36–37), who only does what is expected of everyone? Also, in the case of Ananias and Sapphira (5:1–11), Peter says explicitly that the couple were free to keep their possessions either completely or in part (5:4). No doubt Luke, who wants to hold to his ideal, is not embarrassed by deviations or apparent contradictions. And this ideal, we must reiterate, does not consist of becoming poor but in eradicating the poverty of others.

A few other texts continue the same theme. Acts 11:29

describes how the disciples in Antioch decide to send aid to the brothers and sisters in Rudah, where famine has struck. Luke also mentions the fact that Paul works with his hands in order to help "the weak" (economically), because there is greater happiness in giving than receiving (Paul's discourse at Miletus: Acts 20: 33–35).

Thus even if in Acts, Luke makes no allusion to the sayings of the Lord related in his Gospel or their direct application, he does nonetheless clarify that the reason for renouncing wealth is not asceticism, or scorn for possessions, or the virtue of poverty. Rather, renunciation of material possession creates communion through sharing.

2. THE FATE AND ATTITUDE OF THE DISCIPLE

The portrait of the disciple, as Luke paints it in the different figures throughout Acts, often seems quite close to the portrait depicted in the Gospels.

Paul must suffer on account of Jesus' name (Acts 9:16), endure imprisonment and persecution (20:23), and live in the midst of hardships and tears (20:19). Paul and Barnabas risk their lives for the Lord (15:26). Paul attaches no value to his life (20:24); he is ready to die for Jesus (21:13). Once, after having been flogged, the apostles "left the presence of the Sanhedrin glad to have had the honor of suffering humiliation for the sake of the name" (5:40–41). One has the impression of reading an illustration of the beatitude of those persecuted for the sake of justice (see pp. 106–7).

Stephen, praying for his murderers while he is being stoned (Acts 7:60), is an example of a disciple following the teaching on the love of enemies ("pray for those who persecute you": Matt. 5:44). On the other hand, when Paul was struck on the face he did not turn the other cheek but insulted (without knowing it?) the high priest who had ordered this humiliating punishment (Acts 23:3; cf. Matt.5:39). Finally, Peter is presented as having "neither silver nor gold" (Acts 3:6); Paul declares having desired "no one's silver or gold or apparel" (Acts 20: 33, RSV).

Let us mention fasting (a cultural practice? Acts 13:2; 14:23) and the example of Philip's four daughters in Caesarea who "were virgins and prophets" (Acts 21:9), which quite likely constitutes an allusion to the practice of voluntary celibacy in the primitive community. This would cover most of the passages having some affinity with the radicalism of the Synoptics. The theme of selling one's possessions appears prominently because it is a preliminary condition to *koinonia*, which is, as we have emphasized, contrary to poverty. One likewise sees the disciple persecuted and suffering and yet filled with joy. This brief examination provides a basis for the comparison to which we shall return later.

THE PAULINE CORPUS

Apart from the pastoral letters and the letter to the Hebrews, the Pauline corpus is the most ancient block of New Testament writings. It expresses the faith of Paul and his communities and dates from about A.D. 60. Although his position on various questions is not definitively expressed and some letters are fragmentary, the works nonetheless reveal Paul's global view of the mystery of Christ. Paul understands this mystery (the meaning of Christ's death and resurrection, the effect on the lives of Christians) in a post-Easter light. It is not surprising, then, that traits of Jesus' historical life and reminders of his teachings are almost totally absent in Paul's writings. And yet Paul affirms certain demands concerning the conduct of the Christian which closely resemble some of Jesus' radical sayings as reported by the Synoptics. We shall make a thematic study of these texts.

1. THE BEHAVIOR OF THE APOSTLE

Paul presents the life of the apostles, his own life included, as one of trials and sufferings: often hungry, thirsty, naked, ill-treated, abused, insulted, imprisoned, beaten, poor, without possessions (1 Cor. 4:11; 2 Cor. 6:4–5, 10), and persecuted (2 Cor. 4:9). Another text says that Paul's fate is every Christian's fate (2 Tim. 3:11–12) and that to suffer for the kingdom is a grace (2 Thess. 1:5).

But although Paul is often reduced to a situation of want (Phil. 4:12) and to hard manual labor (1 Cor. 4:12; 9:6), he is occasionally in a state of abundance (Phil. 4:12). He acknowledges that the other apostles have the right to live from their ministry and to be accompanied by a wife (1 Cor. 9:4–7).

2. THE ATTITUDE TOWARD POSSESSIONS[1]

In several letters Paul insists on Christians helping other communities (in Jerusalem) that have material difficulties, which he refers to as "poor" (Rom. 15:26; Gal. 2:10). He organizes a collection on their behalf (Rom. 15:26; 1 Cor. 16:1–4; 2 Cor. 8 and 9). This aid is a voluntary sharing (the word *koinonia* is used with this meaning in Rom. 15:26 and 2 Cor. 8:4) from their abundance—not to burden anyone but "that there may be equality" (2 Cor. 8:12–15, RSV).

In one situation Paul says that when anyone is under instruction in the faith, he should give his teacher a share of all good things he has (Gal. 6:6). In three other letters, a directive is given to attend to the needs of others (Rom. 12:13), share with those in want (Eph. 4:28), and "not neglect to do good and to share (*koinonia*) what you have" (Heb. 13:16, RSV). If one is to believe 1 Corinthians (6:1–8), this sharing does not seem to have been practiced in the community. In fact, some lawsuits were taken to court in order to "wrong and defraud." Also, during the Lord's Supper, there seems to have been discrimination between the rich and "those who have nothing" (1 Cor. 11:21–22).

Finally, it is not impossible that the expression "if I give everything I have to feed the poor" (1 Cor. 13:3) is an allusion to a heroic (and exceptional) act, which was not unknown in the communities and which echoes the Synoptic saying on radical detachment from one's possessions (Mark 10:21).

Two passages in 1 Timothy elaborate at greater length the problem of material possessions and the right use of riches (1 Tim. 6:7–10, 17–19). This letter condemns those who use religion or piety to become wealthy and proposes a completely different behavior. One must be content with what one has: "We have brought nothing into the world, and we can take nothing out of it; but as long as we have food and clothing, let us be content with that" (vv. 7–8). Reminiscent of the wisdom of the somewhat disillusioned sages Job and Qoheleth, but still very true, these verses encourage one to consider oneself happy with the simple necessities of life. Certainly it would be dangerous to insist on a literal meaning; the fact remains, however, that the believer is invited to reduce the level of his or her needs. The one who is content with the minimum essentials is in sharp contrast with the one seeking gain. These moneyseekers "are a prey to temptation; they get trapped into all sorts of foolish and dangerous ambitions which eventually plunge them into ruin and destruction" (6:9).

This almost apocalyptic description (especially because of the words "ruin and destruction") reminds us of the theme of the "seduction of riches" common to the Synoptics (see pp. 74–75). This text ends with a decisive condemnation whose terms are among the harshest in the entire New Testament: "the love of money is the root of all evils" (1 Tim. 6:10a). Those who have surrendered to it stray far from the faith and inflict great grief upon themselves (6:10b). The incompatibility between the desire for riches and salvation faith is illustrated, as we have already pointed out, in the maxim on the two masters (Matt. 6:24; see p. 80).

Another passage from the same letter softens this absolute declaration. There can be good rich people and a proper use of riches (1 Tim. 6:17–19). Three conditions are required for this: (1) not to look down on others; (2) to place one's trust in God, who gives more than we need to be happy (v. 17); and (3) to do good, grow rich in good deeds, give generously and share (v. 18).

In the preceding passage, the love of money was presented as leading to ruin and perdition; here, by sharing, the rich lay "a good foundation for the future, so that they may take hold of the life which is life indeed" (1 Tim. 6:19). One can perceive the parallel with some Synoptic texts: the true treasure (Matt. 6:19–21; see pp. 77–78); the crafty steward (Luke 16:1–9; see p. 86–88). Thus one can be a "good rich person" as long as one depends not on riches but on God and shares with others.

A passage from 2 Corinthians, often presented as a Pauline theology of poverty, deserves our attention. The text (chap. 8) is consecrated to organizing a collection on behalf of the saints in Jerusalem. Paul exhorts the believers of Corinth to be generous. He first proposes to them the model of the faithful of Macedonia whose extreme poverty "overflowed in a wealth of generosity" (2 Cor. 8:2). Paul compliments the Corinthians for their faith, their spiritual gifts of eloquence and understanding, and their charity. He asks them to excel also in generosity (*charis*, 2 Cor. 8:7), following the example of the Lord Jesus Christ whose generosity (*charis*) was manifested by the fact that "he was rich, but he became poor for your sake, to make you rich out of his poverty" (8:9).

What is the meaning of the words "poor" and "poverty" as they appear here? In verse 2 the "intense poverty" of the Macedonians surely describes a socioeconomic situation, but the rhetorical emphasis of the passage (these "poor" people overflow in a wealth of generosity) prevents us from measuring the degree of their poverty. On the other hand, the word can have only a figurative meaning when the subject is Christ becoming poor. In this exhortation to generosity, where Christ is proposed as a model, we have the same theme as found in the famous Christological hymn of Philippians 2:6–11. Christ was rich (his state was divine) but he became poor (he emptied himself). This affirmation describes, through other words and images, the mystery of the incarnation, the suffering and the death of Christ Jesus for the salvation of all.

The categories Paul uses of "poverty/riches" sets the context for him to encourage generous charity on behalf of the poor. Does he, however, by describing the work of salvation as an impoverishment, present a theology of poverty and invite believers to divest themselves materially? It would seem that the example and the exhortation are more oriented toward the notion of generosity than of divestiture.[2]

The eschatological motivations for the attitude of Christians toward material possessions are to be noted. Material possessions (like other human realities such as marriage) are henceforth seen in a new light. Because time is short and the form (*schema*) of this world is passing away (1 Cor. 7:29–31), everything is stripped of its ultimate substance. Thus "those whose life is buying things should live as though they had nothing of their own; and those who have to deal with the world should not become engrossed in it" (1 Cor. 7:30–31). Thus one must not be anxious about material possessions (Phil. 4:6; cf. Matt. 6:25–31). On the contrary, one must be detached from money (1 Tim. 3:3) and shun dishonest gain (1 Tim. 3:8).

3. THE RADICALISM OF LOVE

The love of neighbor, as described in the Sermon on the Mount, must extend even to one's enemies (see pp. 108-9, 112-13, 118-19). One must not judge or resist evil but forgive unceasingly. One encounters the same themes in the Pauline epistles.

Christians are called to bless those who persecute them (Rom. 12:14; 1 Cor. 4:12), to do good to them (Rom. 12:20), to avoid anger (Col. 3:8; Eph. 4:26, 31), to show courtesy to all (Tit. 3:2), not to repay evil for evil (Rom. 12:17; 1 Thess. 5:15). When there is injustice rather than seeking one's rights through lawsuits Paul advises, "Why not rather suffer wrong? Why not rather be defrauded?" (1 Cor. 6:7). Christians must forbear one another (Col. 3:13; Eph. 4:2), carry one another's burdens (Gal. 6:2), refrain from judging (Rom. 14:4,10) set each other right "in a spirit of gentleness" (Gal. 6:2), and correct one another as brother and sister, not as enemies (2 Thess. 3:15). Mutual forgiveness, following the Lords' example, must happen "as soon as a quarrel begins" (Col. 3:13; Eph. 4:32). In order to do this one must "be clothed in sincere compassion, in kindness and humility, gentleness and patience" (Col. 3:12). Such is the agape so lyrically expressed in Paul's letter to the Corinthians: it is not irritable, it does not rejoice at wrong, but bears all things, endures all things (1 Cor. 13: 5-7). The similarities with the Beatitudes and other parts of the Sermon on the Mount are striking.

4. DIVORCE AND VIRGINITY

The rejection of divorce has struck us as one of the radical parts of Jesus' teachings (see pp. 109-11). Not only does Paul continue the same teaching, but he even explicitly refers to one of Jesus' sayings (1 Cor. 7:10). This reference is interesting because it indicates that Paul knew, at least by oral tradition, certain teachings of the historical Jesus. Whatever the case, Paul repeats Jesus' difficult demand while applying it to a concrete situation (1 Cor. 7:10-16).

Paul is also the one who, by virtue of his apostolic responsibility, expressly proposes virginity as a possible charism based on essentially eschatological motivations (1 Cor. 7:25-35). Paul's position, however, has no relation to the logion on eunuchs (see pp. 56–60); on the contrary, Paul specifically denies having any instructions from the Lord on this subject (1 Cor. 7:25).[3]

THE JOHANNINE WRITINGS

In the Johannine writings (the Fourth Gospel, the three letters, Revelation),[4] the radical emphases, such as we have seen in the Synoptics, are almost totally absent. This can be explained by the very special character of these writings, particularly the Gospel in which the author crystallizes a multiplicity of events and sayings into two fundamental points: faith in Jesus and love of neighbor.

There are nonetheless some related passages. While commenting on the Synoptic saying, "Anyone who wants to save his life will lose it (Mark 8:35), we noticed that it could also be found in a somewhat modified form in John 12:25. "Anyone who loves his life loses it; anyone who hates his life in this world will keep it for the eternal life" (See p. 47). This is the only example where John and the Synoptics transmit a saying of Jesus in the same form. A similar expression (on the subject of martyrs—in awkward Greek and with possible Semitic influences) can be found in Revelation (12:11): "for they loved not their lives even unto death" (RSV).

In John 15:13 Jesus speaks about the highest form of love, which consists in giving one's life for one's friends. In 1 John 3:16 it is elaborated: "by this we know love, that he laid down his life for us; and we ought to lay down our lives for the brethren" (RSV). Moreover, the disciple will be hated and persecuted as Jesus was: "the world hates you" (John 15:18); "if they have persecuted me, they will persecute you too" (15:20). "They will expel you from the synagogues . . . anyone who kills you will think he is doing a holy duty for God" (John 16:2); "you will suffer in the world" (16:33, NAB).

On the subject of love, the author affirms that hating one's sister or brother is equal to homicide (1 John 3:15); "to hate your brother is to be a murderer." And also in 1 John 4:20: "anyone who loves God must also love his brother." This absolute call to love one's neighbor even to the point of death is affirmed here in principle, but the very concrete dimension of love through sharing is not neglected (1 John 3:17): "But if any one has the world's goods and sees his brother in need, yet closes his heart against him, how does God's love abide in him?" (RSV).

Concerning the poor, there is in John's Gospel a declaration pronounced by Jesus during the anointing at Bethany (John 12:1–8; cf. also Mark 14:7; Matt. 26:11): "You have the poor with you always, you will not always have me" (v. 8). This saying assumes that the community will always have to take care of the poor. On the other hand, that act does not have exclusive value, for every action done for love of Christ, even if completely lost, has value.

Finally, Revelation (14:4) possibly alludes to the practice of voluntary virginity (of men) in the first century when it speaks of the 144,000 chosen who "have kept their virginity."[5]

THE CATHOLIC EPISTLES

We shall now examine the epistle of James and the first epistle of Peter.

1. JAMES

The resemblance in James to certain themes from the Sermon on the Mount is undeniable. There is in his letter an invective against the rich similar to the "woe to the rich" of Luke's Gospel. In Matthew, the two competing masters are God and money (Matt. 6:24; see p. 80); in James friendship with the world is enmity toward God. Whoever wants to be a friend of the world becomes an enemy of God (Jas. 4:4). James condemns slandering or judging others (4:11; see p. 117–18). It is the only epistle to repeat the interdict against swearing and to affirm the necessity of a frank Yes or No (5:12; cf. Matt. 5:34–37; see also pp. 111–12).

Taking responsibility for the weak (widows and orphans) and an upright conduct (Jas. 1:27) are components of a "pure, unspoilt religion." This help must be concrete: if some are without clothing, one must clothe them; if they have nothing to eat, one must feed them. Otherwise, one's faith is without works and is useless (Jas. 2:14–17).

The poor deserve hospitality and respect, because God chose them "to be rich in faith and to be heirs to the kingdom promised to those who love him" (Jas. 2:5). Understandably, James is extremely hard on the rich, whom this community seems to have favored and flattered at the expense of the poor (Jas. 2:2–3). James warns, "Is it not the rich who oppress you, is it not they who drag you into court? Is it not they who blaspheme that honorable name by which you are called?" (Jas. 2:6–7). It is quite unlikely that this description is addressed to the rich of the community; one thinks, rather, of the powerful of this world who are persecuting the Christians. This must likewise be the case in James 5:1–6, which inveighs against the conduct of the rich and threatens them with the worst misfortune. They have deprived the workers of their salaries; they have lived in comfort and luxury; they have gorged themselves in the time of slaughter; they have condemned and killed the just (vv. 4–6). Woe to them also, for their wealth is rotten, their clothing moth-eaten, their gold and silver corroded. The cries of the oppressed have reached the ears of the Lord of hosts. The rich have prepared the fire that will consume them (vv. 2–3).

A small hope remains all the same for rich Christians: if they become aware of the fragility of their wealth, if they know how to glory in their "humiliation," they will be able to share in the exaltation of those of humble condition (Jas. 1:9–10).

2. 1 PETER

Three passages in 1 Peter echo the Beatitude of the persecuted: it is a grace to endure unjust suffering (1 Pet. 2:19–20). "If you have to suffer for justice' sake, happy will you be" (3:14, NAB); "rejoice insofar as you share Christ's sufferings. . . . If you are reproached for the name of Christ, you are blessed" (4:13–14).

Fraternal love calls for compassion and mercy. One must not repay evil for evil or insult for insult, but rather, one must bless the offenders (1 Pet. 3:8–9).

Addressing himself to the elders who exercise authority, Peter makes this recommendation (5:3): "be examples to your flock, not lording it over those assigned to you" (NAB). The expression translated here as "lording it over" (*katakyrieuo*: to dominate, rule as a despot or master) is exactly the same as the word used in the logion "among the Gentiles those who seem to exercise authority lord it over them" (Mark 10:42, NAB; see p. 38). The apostles must absolutely avoid imitating those rulers. It is difficult not to see an allusion here in word and meaning to this saying of Jesus.

GENERAL CONCLUSION

The texts presented in this chapter are not found in well-defined groups but are spread out here and there throughout the New Testament. We have analyzed them according to the order of the books in which they are found. Now it is possible to reassemble them for a more complete synthesis. In our opinion, these texts revolve around one of three major themes: (1) the suffering and happiness of the disciple, (2) the radicality of love, and (3) possessions.

1. THE SUFFERING AND HAPPINESS OF THE DISCIPLE

This theme echoes Jesus' announcement of persecution and proclamation of blessings for those who suffer. It no doubt reveals the very real opposition that the early Christians encountered.

The book of Acts describes Stephen's and Paul's experiences in terms of sufferings and joy. Paul himself presents his life as filled with trials and sufferings, and yet these sufferings are a source of joy. All Christians, moreover, who are destined to suffer and be put to death (Acts, John, Peter) are proclaimed blessed. The testimony of the martyrs no doubt substantiates these declarations. The community thus believed that Jesus' promise, noted in John's Gospel and the Synoptics, was being actualized: "anyone who hates his life in this world will keep it for the eternal life" (John 12:25).

2. THE RADICALITY OF LOVE

The writings that we have just analyzed contain most of the radical traits of the love of neighbor: the love of enemies and persecutors (Acts, Paul); not repaying evil for evil (Paul, Peter); mutual support and forgiveness (Paul); the refusal to judge (Paul, James), which supposes mercy and tenderness (Paul, Peter). John, who equates hate with homicide, introduces the notion of giving one's life for one's brother or sister.

3. POSSESSIONS

In the Synoptics the question of possessions and their use occupies an important place (see chap. 5). In other New Testament writings—and this comes perhaps as a surprise—this theme is also highlighted to some extent. As a matter of fact, almost all the dimensions of this question are present with, of course, nuances, peculiar to each writing style.

Sharing (Koinonia)

The Synoptics insist on sharing with the poor, though apart from the instance of Zacchaeus no concrete examples are given. The practice of the first communities reveals to us how this sharing—this *koinonia*—was actualized. In Acts the Jerusalem community practiced it totally. The ideal is, in fact, qualified by other factors. At any rate, mutual help between communities did seem to prevail. Such a viewpoint also emerges from Paul's letters: even if none of his churches practiced commonality, the duty to share and to help one another was generally fulfilled, especially toward the mother church in Jerusalem. We find the same concern in James and even John (1 John), a concern not to become poor, but rather, to create equality.

The Danger of Riches

Acts and the major Pauline letters present people belonging to the rich and upper classes of society who are converts and collaborators of the apostle.[6] Contrary to what is found in the Synoptics, no criticism of riches or the rich can be found in these writings. On the other hand, vehement criticism is expressed in James and 1 Timothy. James, using language worthy of an Amos or an Isaiah, attacks the rich, the oppressors, the exploiters and denounces their rotting riches. No less vigorous is the condemnation of the greedy person in 1 Timothy: the love of money is the root of all evil (6:7–10).

"Good" Rich People

These writings offer, however, a counterpart to the absolutism that could result from this position. Rich people may be "good" if they place their trust in God, humble themselves, and above all give and share. As we have said, Acts especially shows people who are not poor, yet who are counted among Paul's friends.

The Poor and Poverty

James' eulogy of the poor is completely in line with the Lucan Beatitudes (see pp. 75–77). John mentions the inevitable presence of the poor in the community. The first letter to Timothy is the only writing in the New Testament that proposes in a polemical manner what could be referred to as a "strict use" of material possessions: to be content with food and clothing. This text comes the closest to idealizing poverty. Paul speaks about the poverty of the apostle, but it is far more than mere material indigence, for he knows how to face "abundance and want" (Phil. 4:12). He affirms the ephemeral character of the goods of this world and whatever is related to them. This eschatological motif does not explicitly appear in the Synoptics. Finally, we have noted Paul's use of binomials (rich/poor, enrich/impoverish) to express the mystery of Christ, the source of riches and liberality, humbling himself.

4. MISCELLANEOUS POINTS

The rejection of divorce is reaffirmed by Paul. He also attests to and justifies the practice of voluntary celibacy. Texts in Acts and Revelation suggest, to say the least, the existence of this practice in the communities. Fasting, likewise, is mentioned, often in relation to celebration (Acts). As for Paul's mention of fasting, it is difficult to say if he considers it a voluntary practice or a necessity. Finally, two points of contact with the Synoptic texts should be noted: the elders of the community are told not "to lord it over" those in their care (1 Peter). All Christians are warned against oath-taking (James).

5. DIFFERENCES AND SILENCES

Evaluating the differences between these texts and the Synoptics is not easy because of the variety of literary styles, original settings, aims, and dates. Although one of these writings is a Gospel (John), it is still profoundly different in structure and even more so in content. The other books contain messages elicited by particular situations (the various letters). Only Acts can be understood as following Luke's Gospel; but it nevertheless covers a completely different area.

Having said this, we are struck by the continuity we find. In fact, most of the themes transmitted by the Synoptics find parallels in one or another of these writings. Can one even speak of differences? Thus every time the theme of love of neighbor is broached, a harmony of content and a convergence of form can be found.

It is in the area of sharing that one can detect considerable differences. The poor are proclaimed blessed (but only by James), and distrust of money is confirmed (1 Timothy, James). However, the invitation to divest oneself of one's possessions on behalf of the poor, so strongly affirmed in the Synoptics, is nowhere repeated. What does appear is the sharing of possessions within the community (Jerusalem) and the often repeated demand for mutual aid among individuals or communities. Is there a relationship between the "communism" of Jerusalem and the call of Jesus? Is Paul, who is seemingly unaware of this type of sharing, equally unaware of the tradition transmitted by the Synoptics? For the moment it suffices to raise the question. It is important for us but does not seem to be a preoccupation of the Pauline communities.

As far as the silences are concerned, let us first point out the absence of the theme of "following Christ," with the concrete demands that this implies: abandoning one's trade and possessions and severing family ties. Understandably, the situation of believers after Easter did not allow for the same actions. We see the apostles traveling in the company of their wives and being supported by their ministry. The phrase "the workman deserves his keep" is the only one explicitly retained from the discourse on mission (Matt. 10:10 and 1 Cor. 9:14).

One does not perceive any direct references to the sayings that we assembled in chapter 7 concerning the difficulty of the undertaking confronting followers of Jesus. Some demands, radical in content, are presented but not set in opposition to the Mosaic Law (as in the antitheses we discussed, see pp. 107–16), since the issues did not arise in these terms.

Having reached the end of this comparison, let us emphasize the fact that although the Pauline corpus contains numerous parallels with the radicalism in the Synoptics, this is not the case for the Johannine writings. We have noted only rare similarities.

In conclusion, we think that this textual analysis, which certainly is not complete, has presented almost all the Synoptic passages fitting our definition of "radical." We have even widened our inquiry, though only summarily, to include similar texts in other New Testament writings. Usually each chapter and each significant subgroup was followed by a conclusion synthesizing the essence of the analysis. This overlapping repetition seemed useful to clarify our subject matter and for pedagogical purposes.

At the risk of retracing our steps, we must now condense the general conclusions of our study. This repetition, or overview, rather than engendering saturation or tedium should allow us to see more clearly this complex subject matter.

NOTES

1. A good presentation can be found in Ph. Seidensticker, "Saint Paul et la pauvreté," *La pauvreté évangélique,* 27, in Lire la Bible (Paris: Cerf, 1971), pp. 93–133.

2. "The point of the example proposed to the Corinthians is not the imitation of the poverty of Christ, which is a figurative description of his Incarnation, but the imitation of the *charis* of Christ, the love which enriches others" (Seidensticker, "Saint Paul," p. 110).

3. For Paul's position on marriage and celibacy, see X. Léon-Dufour, "Mariage, et continence selon Saint Paul," *A la rencontre de*

Dieu, Mémorial Albert Gelin (Lyon: X. Mappus, 1961), pp. 319–29.

4. This convenient collection does not imply that a position is taken on the identity of the author of the Gospel and of Revelation.

5. For indications of different possible exegetical interpretations, see Matura, "Le célibat dans le Nouveau Testament d'après l'exégèse récente," *Nouvelle Revue Théologique* 97 (1975): 598–99.

6. Lydia, in the purple-dye trade, Acts 16:14; some prominent women, Acts 17:4–5; Dionysius the Areopagite and Damaris, Acts 17:34; Crispus, ruler of the synagogue, Acts 18:7–8; Crispus, Gaius, Stephanas, Chloe, 1 Cor. 1:11, 14, 16; Erastus, the city treasurer, Rom. 16:23. See Seidensticker, "Saint Paul," p. 115.

PART THREE

**OVERVIEW
AND
OPEN QUESTIONS**

9

The Content of Radicalism according to the Synoptics

In the first part of this study we presented radical Synoptic texts in two different frameworks: a topical classification and a textual classification (see chap. 2). As we reach the conclusion of our analysis we see the texts forming complementary groupings.

TWO PRESENTATIONS OF RADICALISM

The radical passages can be presented in two manners: assembled around certain central, connecting ideas or according to common areas of application.

1. FOUR POLES OF RADICAL THOUGHT

Following Jesus

In order to become a disciple of Jesus (first of all in the historical period, then as believers after Easter), one must deny oneself, take up one's cross, and so forth, that is, encounter opposition, division, persecution, and even death. To walk in Jesus' footsteps requires leaving family, possessions, and profession. While on mission the disciples have no baggage, are without any security, and thus must count on God and the hospitality of those to whom they bring the good news.

The most radical of the demands (acceptance of suffering and death receives greater emphasis than leaving possessions or next of kin) gravitates around the idea of following Jesus. This is shown in the texts analyzed in chapter 3.

Love

Other demands focus on the love of neighbor. To love one's brother and sister means not to judge or condemn them but, rather, to forgive and be reconciled with them, to avoid bad feelings and harsh words—in short, to manifest the tenderness of God. Even when the brother or sister becomes an enemy, love must remain sincere and concrete, submitting to violence without resisting it if necessary. This is the message of the Beatitudes in Matthew: the meek, gentle, merciful, and the peacemakers are those who commit themselves to the service of love. Finally, within the community, where structures, responsibilities, and some forms of authority are inevitable, true greatness will be measured by the desire for service and humility. It is the least, the weakest who is the greatest (see pp. 34–41, 102–7).

Unpretentiousness

The kingdom is proclaimed and given to the poor, to those who hunger and thirst for it, who weep and suffer until it comes, who are powerless and defenseless as children. For only what is empty will be filled. Surely, works of justice are required—for God alone and not to be seen by others—for only the pure of heart (upright and faithful) will see God. Yet no matter what disciples do, they will always be "useless servants" and will never make God indebted to them. To be perpetually poor and defenseless before God is a difficult endeavor. But the urgency of the situation demands that one risk everything. And the last word will always be from God, who makes the sun rise on the bad as well as the good (see pp. 36–47, 103–7, 128–42).

Sharing

Our texts consistently represent riches as a permanent danger, but nowhere do we find material poverty valued in itself or explicitly proposed as an ascetical practice.

The rich person (and ultimately everyone) must be suspicious of money and possessions to which one can easily become enslaved and in which one is tempted to place one's trust. The call to sell everything must always be seen in the perspective of giving, distributing, and sharing. In the Gospels the command is heard (and for Zacchaeus, the decision is made), but the practical response is not given.

Acts gives an ideal image of what was attempted. Paul's letters modestly attest to it. They also talk about help between communities rather than total material commonality. In short, if one goes strictly by the Gospel texts, one would hear less about poverty and more about sharing as a means of alleviating the needs of others and creating equality.

2. AREAS OF APPLICATION

The demands of Jesus address the concrete behavior of the person. When they require an especially strong effort or extraordinary kind of conduct, they are said to be radical. This radicality applies to two different areas, the inner life and outer material possessions.

In the first category are three of the demands articulated above: to follow Jesus, to love, to avoid pretentiousness. Certainly the decision to follow Jesus—implying detachment, love of neighbor, renouncing claims on God and on divine rewards—requires visible responses and undertakings. The fact remains that, aside from some exceptions, this first category refers essentially to inner attitudes and relationships with God and neighbor.

The second category of outer radicalism essentially concerns material possessions. The prescriptions, which encourage a break between the person and his or her possessions, are visible and more daring in their radicalism than the preceding category. To renounce oneself, lose one's life, love one's enemies, refrain from judging—all these are less immediately visible than the act of surrendering one's possessions to the poor. Moreover, the result of the latter action can more or less be measured, which is not the case, for example, with forgiveness.

Even if not completely comparable with possessions, the severance of family ties (leaving parents, brothers, sisters, children, and spouse) and renouncing marriage (which the text on eunuchs suggests, Matt. 19:12) could also be categorized as "outer" radicalism.

The distinction established here is not arbitrary. We shall see that most problems and difficulties of interpretation and practice of gospel radicality are traceable to this last category.

RADICALISM—LITERAL OR FIGURATIVE?

Bearers of unusual demands, the radical sayings often appear in quite unusual literary forms. They use paradox, exaggeration, striking images. It is useful to sketch quickly a typology of these forms in order to understand the particular way each demand is expressed.

Let us begin with the images that clearly cannot be taken literally. To tear out one's eye, cut off one's hand or foot, become a eunuch, carry one's cross, become like a child—these expressions, as already explained during our study, are designed, by means of sharp images, to inculcate a type of behavior demanded in the context.

Other images could very well be more than simply literary forms and may be taken literally in some circumstances, for example: nonresistance; going the second mile; letting everything you have be taken. This is even clearer for the following: to renounce oneself, hate oneself, lose oneself. These are not simply images but bare demands that cannot be explained away but remain universally and immediately applicable.

Some direct demands have a juridical appearance. Such is the case for the interdict on divorce (see pp. 109–11) and Jesus' command to the rich man, "Go, sell what you have and give it to the poor" (see pp. 62–68), repeated by Luke in other contexts (see p. 94). These are not exhortations to optional actions but categorical declarations, orders.

Only the saying on eunuchs is presented as an invitation to those who can understand it, because they have been given the capacity to do so (Matt. 19:12). It is the only "counsel," if we may use this word so full of ambiguity.

One can see that it is impossible to reduce the radicalism to literary paradox. After having given due thought to the forms and images, the demands appear all the more sharply. The believing reader is challenged and cannot use a literary pretext to escape from the demands.

RADICALISM AND THE SYNOPTIC MESSAGE
AS A WHOLE

The preceding analyses have strongly insisted on certain aspects of the ethical teachings of Jesus transmitted by the Synoptics. In so doing we made huge gaps in the total message, which could leave an unbalanced presentation. Thus it is necessary to situate, even if summarily, these radical demands in relationship to the totality of the message. This is a difficult task, for it forces us to schematize drastically the diverse points of the message that each redactor considers fundamental.

It seems to us that the Synoptic message revolves around the proclamation of the kingdom, the manifestation of the Father and his tenderness toward his people, and the presentation of Jesus as herald and fulfillment of salvation. Jesus' mission begins by preaching the nearness of the kingdom of God; to receive it, one must be converted, radically change one's life (*metanoia*), and believe in the coming new reality (Mark 1:14–15). Numerous passages, especially the parables, emphasize the urgency of time, the necessity of making a decision, the power of the Word (see the section on parables in Matt. 13), and vigilance (see the parables on vigilance, Matt. 24:37–25:30).

This coming of the reign of God, this new situation that over-turns established structures and positions is ultimately God him-self manifesting to the world his tender and gracious face. The poor, in every meaning of the word, the needy, the little ones, the weak, the sick, the sinners, the marginal ones, rejected and scorned by society—in short, all those who acknowledge their need for salvation—are the beneficiaries of this unconditional ac-tion of God who is like a Father to them (see the Beatitudes; the texts on the reception of sinners, Matt. 2:5, 7; the Lucan parables on mercy, Luke 15).

Jesus is the one who establishes the reign. Where he is present, where his miracles unfold, the kingdom enters into the world (Matt. 12:28; Luke 17:21). The three evangelists focus their narratives on him, each in his own way. Mark's Gospel describes the power and miracles of the Son of God. For Matthew, Jesus is the new Moses, giving a law of grace to his disciples. Luke sees in

Jesus the revelation of the mercy of the Father. All three give us a glimpse into the inexpressible mystery that he embodies, and which unfolds in stages: baptism, temptation, transfiguration, agony, passion, death, empty tomb, and post-resurrection appearances.

The hearers of Jesus (and of the Gospels) are drawn into a completely new situation in which they must henceforth behave as God would, by being perfect as he is perfect (Matt. 5:48). The demands for new modes of conduct flow from that divine example and surpass by far the old codes of justice (Matt. 5:20 and the six antitheses that follow). The crux is the double commandment of love of God and neighbor (Mark 12:28-31).

It is with this general background in mind that we must consider what is said here on radicalism. We see more clearly now how the demands of radicalism are connected with a new type of existence with its harsh realities and cutting edge. But these demands are not the totality or even (at least not always) the most important point. We would greatly err if we thought that in the teaching of Jesus as presented by the Synoptics there is a common undemanding basis to which "radical" commands are occasionally added. The fact is that this basis, of which we have not explicitly spoken, entails the most difficult demands. To be converted, to reorient one's life completely, to receive Jesus' message fully, "to believe in the gospel" (Matt. 1:15), to remain watchful, to pursue Jesus' secret, which dramatically unfolds in the scandal of opposition, suffering, and death—this lies at the very heart of the believer's existence as presented by the Synoptics.

The radical sayings are only condensed and crystallized intransigent formulas about *metanoia* (conversion) and the commandment "You will love the Lord your God with all your heart . . . and your neighbor as yourself." These are such demanding outward projections that one's entire self is gripped; one rises above oneself, one's life, and one's death. The demand for conversion, belief, love, and vigilance goes without saying. The love commandment has no blunt words or expressions. Compared to the radical sayings, it might seem to state only generalities when in fact it is so radically at the root of those demands that without it they have no meaning. (Some demands, however, such as the call to hate one's life in order to find it, directly touch this essential point.)

One must never separate these two dimensions. Radicalism, if detached from the basis that we have just described, quickly becomes rigid, narrow, ascetic feats. Conversion, faith in Jesus, and love of others when stripped of their radical application are diluted to mere theories. Our initial focus, as presented in the beginning, has limited our study to a particular point of view. It is all the more necessary to point out that our approach needs to be situated and completed: radicalism has meaning only if related to the totality of the ethical demands, which we have only glimpsed here.[1]

THE SPECIAL PROBLEM OF THE RADICALISM OF POSSESSIONS

We have already noted the special problem raised by what we at one point called "radicalism of sharing" and at another point "outer radicalism." That collection of texts speaks of not trusting in possessions, of surrendering them to the poor, and also of severing family ties.

It is striking to observe the numerical importance of the texts on this theme. Chapter 5, which reports and analyzes them, is the longest one of our study. It is as if the difficulties of putting such instructions into practice required presenting them in a variety of ways.

When trying to interpret related passages or to specify the recipients of the message (not to mention the current applications), one has the impression that all the questions return to the issue of radicalism. Did Jesus truly require such radical actions? To whom were they proposed? How did the evangelists understand them and whom did they have in mind? These questions arise, as we have seen, for the major texts: the demands addressed to three potential disciples (see pp. 30–31) and the narrative of the rich man (see pp. 62–68). Some textual uncertainties still exist because, although the calls seem absolute, the response is relative. Thus the twelve who, in order to follow Jesus, leave everything—family and possessions—conserve their family bonds. Some further disparities manifest themselves in the description of the ideal total material sharing of the faithful in Jerusalem.

Thus, strangely enough, it is not the infinitely stronger demands (deny oneself, carry one's cross, lose oneself, hate one's life, etc.) that arouse questions. There is agreement on both what they mean—they require death to self and, should the occasion arise, the acceptance of physical death for the sake of Jesus—and to whom they are directed: all those who assent to faith in Jesus.

Less important than others, the "outer," immediately concrete demands are especially verifiable and permanent. One either leaves behind one's possessions and family or one does not. This can be identified, whereas death to self is an indefinite process that cannot be measured—and one does not physically die every day.

We shall have to return again to this subject; let it suffice for the moment to have raised the issue.

NOTE

1. Percy, *Die Botschaft Jesu* (Lund: C. W. K. Gleerup, 1953); Schnackenburg, *The Moral Teaching of the New Testament* (New York: Herder and Herder, 1965 and Crossroad, 1973); and Neuhäusler, *Exigence de Dieu et Morale chrétienne* (Paris: Cerf, 1971) present an overview of the demands of Jesus, but their study of radicalism is much too limited.

10

The Motives of Radicalism

One does not accept the difficult modes of conduct required by
Jesus and his teaching in a gratuitous way or for arbitrary reasons. When classifying Jesus' demands around certain poles of
thought (adherence to Jesus, love of neighbor, and sharing), we
suggested some possible reasons for obeying such extraordinary
demands. We shall again, in a more systematic manner, study the
motivations that the evangelists explicitly or implicitly equate
with certain radical actions.

"FOR MY SAKE"

When Jesus desired a few disciples to "be with him" (Mark
3:14; 5:18), his decisive call was "Follow me" (Mark 1:12). To
walk in Jesus' footsteps, to be his disciple by sharing his life, his
mission, and his fate is the root and the source of one's concrete
actions. To leave one's family—to "hate" them, neglect the most
basic duties toward them—and be ready for martyrdom is necessary if one wants to be "worthy" of him (Matt. 10:37–38) or simply to be his "disciple" (Luke 14:26–27, 33). Thus most of the
demands addressed to the "disciples" are based on the desire to
"be with him" (see chaps. 3–4). And these are the strongest demands: renouncing oneself, one's natural bonds and one's possessions, and accepting violent death.

If one considers the Synoptic presentation, one notices that the
description of the "historical vocations" contains only the invita-

tion "Follow me." No other demand is mentioned; surrendering everything, which follows, seems to come on its own (see pp. 28–30). Three "ideal" scenes (discussed on pp. 30–31) give details on the required renunciations: to be ready for insecurity; "let [immediately] the dead bury their dead." The more extensive collections on renunciation also emphasize the cost of discipleship (see pp. 45–56).

The vocation narratives do not explicitly say why the disciples immediately answered Jesus' call, but the implied reason is that they wanted to be with Jesus and to follow in his footsteps. The texts on renunciation directly affirm that it is because of Jesus (Mark 8:35; 10:29), on account of his name (Matt. 19:29), the gospel (only Mark 8:35), the kingdom (Matt. 19:12), and in order to be a disciple and be worthy of him that one accepts his demands and acts on them.

Thus no matter how one views the demands of discipleship, one observes that they are all connected to the person of Jesus. The texts do not describe—out of discretion or modesty?—the bonds or actions between the disciples and Jesus. Neither faith nor love is mentioned; it is only said that everything is possible—including the highest renunciation: death—because of Jesus.

And this is how one must understand both the disciples' historical situation of being grasped by the call and the situation of the Christian believer whose life is centered on the Lord Jesus. The basis of radicalism is, first, to value Jesus unconditionally, above all else.

"BE COMPASSIONATE AS YOUR FATHER IS COMPASSIONATE"

Some radical demands presented concern the relationship between the person and his or her neighbor. What we are trying to see is what is behind these demands: to become nothing and a servant; to share with the poor; to avoid anger and offending others; not to judge; to forgive; to endure violence and persecution; to love one's enemies and to do good to them; to be gentle, a peacemaker, and compassionate (see chap. 6).

We must acknowledge that most of these commandments are not explained by explicit motivations. Some (e.g., the antitheses; see pp. 107–16) are simply presented as laws, which are reaffirmed or established by the sovereign, supreme authority of Jesus for his disciples. Others are accompanied by apparently self-seeking reasons: one must not judge, since one is a sinner and will also be judged; one must give so that others may give to us; one must forgive in order to be forgiven by God. Silhouetted behind these motivations is the Golden Rule (Matt. 7:12): "So always treat others as you would like them to treat you."

But there is something deeper. A more radical motive is indicated in a text that concludes a teaching in Matthew/Luke on the love of enemies (Matt. 5:48; Luke 6:36, which in the Lucan version reads: "Be compassionate as your Father is compassionate."

The only reason to love others as God loves everyone—the good and the bad, the just and the unjust (Matt. 5:45)—is love itself. Jesus calls his disciples to behave as God does, to be "perfect" (Matt. 5:48) as God is perfect. According to Matthew (the only one to use this rare word), perfection consists in loving unselfishly with a readiness to sacrifice. By loving in this way (are we not affirming here something nearly impossible?) the person penetrates into the depths where the very love of God is communicated to him or her. Such is the ultimate motive, the root, and the possibility of love for one another.

VARIOUS MOTIVES

In addition to these all-encompassing motivations, we can also mention other startling ones. Certain attitudes or radical actions are conditions for obtaining life (Mark 9:43; 10:17) or entering into the kingdom (Mark 9:47; Matt. 18:3) and are indispensable elements for an integrated whole life of the disciple (Matt. 19:21). Thus it is better to lose parts of one's body than to lose one's life and the kingdom. Also, to possess life, to be "perfect," one must sell all and give to the poor.

These motives are related to the motive of reward, such as treasure in heaven (Mark 10:21; Matt. 6:2, 4, 6, 18–21). Everything surrendered because of Jesus will be restored a hundred times over (Mark 10:30) and deeds done in secret, before God alone, will be rewarded. Finally, the Beatitudes, especially the Matthean version, offer the prospect of future happiness for those who live the gospel.

Warnings about material possessions emphasize the dangers to those who have them. It is difficult for the rich to enter into the kingdom (Mark 10:23), for riches seduce (Mark 4:19), enslave (Matt. 6:24), and close one's heart to others (Luke 16:19-31). One also must be circumspect in using them (Luke 16:9). After such negative remarks one would expect the conclusion: rid yourselves of riches as soon as possible. Instead, Jesus invites one to give, distribute, and share (Luke 6:34-35, 38; 11:41). Possessions in themselves are not evil, only their egotistical, selfish, and excessive use.

Before leaving on mission the disciples are instructed to reduce their equipment to the minimum (see pp. 31-34). The reason behind this is not immediately evident. Is traveling light meant to facilitate speed or emphasize the detachment of the missionary? Or is it not, rather, a simple committing of oneself to the kind hospitality of others in faith that one will lack nothing?

ESCHATOLOGICAL MOTIVATIONS

Among the radical texts analyzed in Part Two, are there some of an eschatological nature? In other words, do some of the demands regarding behavior spring from the expectation of the coming end of time? Would Jesus (or the community) have proposed extreme (even impossible) modes of conduct out of a mentality that "the end times with their horrors and harsh trials are imminent"?[1]

Our analysis does not orient us in this direction. Nothing in the texts or in their immediate contexts supports such a perspective. The disciple's decisions are made in relation to Jesus' call concerning the right use of possessions, transcending the Law, and the urgency of the situation. This situation marks the coming of the reign of God, present in the person and actions of Jesus.

Thus everything depends on the interpretation of the statement "the time has come . . . and the kingdom of God is close at hand" (Mark 1:15). If we adopted the hypothesis that Jesus proclaimed and expected the imminent end of this world and the definitive advent of a new age, we would be of the opinion that "these extreme demands form . . . a provisional ethic."[2] If, however, we accept the hypothesis that Jesus inaugurated a reign whose time limits were not set and whose horizon of fulfillment remained unknown, we would see the radical demands as related to the present and as eschatological only in an incipient sense.

The fact remains, as we have noted, that except for three radical texts evoking the coming of the Son of man in glory (Matt. 25:31–45; Mark 8:38) and assuring that some will not die before having seen the reign of God (Mark 9:1), one does not find any clear indications of an eschatological orientation (see p. 50). The emphasis is different, of course, for Paul, who affirms that "the form of this world is passing away" (1 Cor. 7:29–31, RSV), thus justifying Christian detachment concerning marriage and possessions (see p. 150). But in the Synoptics the ephemeral character of this world is not directly emphasized or presented as a motive for one's actions.

NOTES

1. Schnackenburg, *The Moral Teaching of the New Testament* (New York: Herder and Herder, 1965 and Crossroad, 1973), p. 81, expounding upon A. Schweitzer's "provisional ethic," an ethic dictated by the expectation of an imminent end of the world.

2. Ibid.

11

The Recipients of the Message of Radicalism

The issue of the recipients of Jesus' message of radicalism is a crucial one, since problems arise for those particularly affected. When analyzing the texts we have tried to raise this issue consistently. Now we shall try to synthesize all the material.

THE EVENTS

Holding the middle ground between a fundamentalism that would read the Gospels as historical narrative and a skepticism that would see them as didactic writings without any foundation in actual events, we think that a certain amount of objective historical data support the narratives. This position enables us to address the question, Whom did Jesus ask to make radical choices?

1. DEMANDS OF THE DISCIPLES

When we say "disciples" we mean the group who followed Jesus and formed a sort of community with him ("the twelve"). Personally called by Jesus to follow him, they left their trades and their families in order to share his itinerant life and mission. We have already noted that in the narratives of personal vocations no demand is imposed other than following Jesus. Their acts of abandonment are mentioned as logical consequences of their choices (see pp. 28–30); when they are sent forth on mission they are instructed to divest themselves and travel light, depending on the hospitality of their hearers for food and lodging. When power conflicts take place among them, Jesus impresses upon them the necessity of service and that the least among them would be the greatest. Finally, persecutions, sufferings, and possible death are announced to them. These, then, are the radical instructions addressed to the twelve that we can assume have a sound historical basis.[1]

2. UNIVERSAL DEMANDS

What can be said, then, about the general demands of renunciation of one's life, family, and particularly one's possessions (see chaps. 4–5)? Were such demands formulated by Jesus and for whom were they intended?

To "hate" one's life, to deny oneself, carry one's cross, and love Jesus more than those closest to us are demands that could have been directed toward the limited group of disciples. But it is difficult to reserve those demands exclusively to them. The aim of such renunciation is universal and the application to all believers is quite natural.

The question of abandonment of possessions presents special difficulties, particularly when determining its significance and who was to be included on the historical level. The vocation narratives, which certainly present a kernel of historical truth, never explicitly demand selling one's possessions. The only occasion when such a deed is linked to the twelve is the pericope on the reward promised for detachment (Mark 10:28–31; see pp. 69–73). There the renunciation is total, including the family as well as possessions. Moreover, the point of the pericope ("there is no one who has left . . . who will not be repaid . . .") and Peter's affirmation ("we have left everything . . .") seem to be redactional padding.

Thus the question arises: Did Jesus require possessions to be abandoned (or better, shared) and was this demand restricted or universal? We have seen that the saying "Sell what you have" (Mark 10:21) can be found in three different forms and contexts: in the particular episode of the rich man, common to the Synoptics (see pp. 62–68), and twice in Luke, presented there with universal nuances (Luke 12:33; 14:33; see pp. 54, 85).

Admittedly it is difficult to determine with any certitude the underlying historical kernel. The case of the rich man could plausibly have been a historical occasion for a general declaration by Jesus that the well-to-do must share with the poor. Luke, especially sensitive to this dimension, not only preserved the concrete example but also repeated the declaration in different ways. Attributing the demand to Jesus seems all the more likely to us because the community did not practice it easily or naturally, as Paul's letters and Acts testify. Consequently, it is difficult to credit its creation to a "communist" tendency of the community or of Luke himself. To whom can it be traced? We think we can find an echo of a saying of Jesus affirming the necessity of sharing, and addressing by means of a possible historical case the totality of believers.

The general counsels on the detached use of possessions (see chap. 5), the Beatitudes, the Sermon on the Mount (see chap. 6), and the sayings on the difficulty of the undertaking (see chap. 7), inasmuch as they retain the substance of Jesus' preaching, seem to be directed to all historical hearers, whether they be immediate disciples or not.

We must repeat that we still remain hesitant regarding the problem of abandoning (or sharing) possessions. We do not really know if the difficulty resides in the texts or if we are merely frightened by the consequences. These consequences are very different, depending on whether Jesus demands a particular personal decision or proposes a universal rule of conduct.

THE REDACTION

We have tried to establish—to be sure hypothetically—to whom the radical demands of Jesus were addressed. From there, one could attempt to find out how these demands were applied (and modified) in the concrete experience of the communities, which in a Jewish or a Gentile setting received the Christian preaching. But such an undertaking goes beyond the framework we have set for ourselves. Also, putting aside the complex and hypothetical "history of traditions," let us move directly to the redactional work—that is, the presentation of facts and sayings—of the evangelist-redactors.

Who, precisely, are the recipients of the radical instructions in the Synoptics? How, in what context, and to whom do Mark, Matthew, and Luke present the logia of Jesus—logia that they received from a tradition already oriented in a certain direction?

For greater clarity we shall first indicate what seems to us to be the redactionally undebatable positions concerning cases that do not apply beyond that particular historical situation. Second, we shall locate the instructions and universal demands undeniably addressed to all hearers of the message. Finally, we shall discuss the cases subject to divergent interpretations because they appear both particular and universal.

1. PARTICULAR DEMANDS

The Synoptics relate accounts of personal vocations as chosen by the twelve (see pp. 28–30). They describe their mission with its special demands, announce their fate, and prescribe what their attitude of service should be. These demands are certainly related to concrete historical situations: Simon and Andrew, James and John (Mark 1:16–20), and Levi (Mark 2:13–14) really follow Jesus and, consequently, make certain breaks with their past.

Each evangelist has his own way of situating the narrative. Luke insists on the absolute character of these breaks ("they left everything," Luke 5:11, 28), and he widens the concept of mission by increasing the number in his mission narrative to seventy-two disciples (Luke 10:1–12). When the evangelists relate the call of the disciples and report the special instructions that they received, they are undeniably remembering remarkable teachings that, by themselves, do not have universal significance. They were teachings given primarily, if not exclusively, to the original actors. We need to acknowledge that those experiences of the past were colored by what had happened since to the twelve and to other preachers and missionaries of the community. But the narratives from the past are not simply memories; they strongly invite the hearers and the readers to relive in a different historical situation (Jesus is no longer there; no one can literally follow in his footsteps) something of the same demands.

2. UNIVERSAL DEMANDS

On the redactional level, the great majority of demands do not solicit a particular group of people but, rather, all those who listen to Jesus' words. The general demands of renunciation have a universal audience ("the disciples and the crowd," Mark 8:34; "everyone," Luke 9:23; "a great crowd," Luke 14:25; see also chap. 4, above), as do almost all the texts on possessions (see chap. 5), on the radicalization of the law (see chap. 6), and on the difficulty of the undertaking (see chap. 7). The only exception—which we would not hesitate to call a "counsel," if this word was not so theologically charged and ambiguous—is the logion on eunuchs, which proposes possible celibacy for the sake of the kingdom for those "who can understand it" (Matt. 19:12; see pp. 56–60). We have referred to this passage many times. Let us be content here with reaffirming that, apart from what concerned the disciples in the strict and limited sense, the Gospel redactors viewed the radical demands of Jesus as applying to everyone who wishes to hear them.

3. DEBATED TEXTS

What remains are three texts that, initially, do not fit any of the categories above. These are, in the triple tradition, the narrative of the rich man and the two pericopes that follow (Mark 10:17–31; see pp. 62–73); in Matthew/Luke the two anonymous disciples (Matt. 18:22; see pp. 30–31); and finally, in Luke the twice-repeated command to "sell what you have" (Luke 12:33; 14:33). As one can see, these texts essentially have the common theme of material possessions.

These texts do not all fit in the category of "universal demands," since they address very specific situations: a man, anonymous disciples. The individuals, however, are left in the shadows, seemingly paradigms or models rather than historical remembrances. It is important to situate them precisely, since, paradoxically, radicalism on the use of material possessions is extended to them. If there are special cases—narratives on vocations—that have been lost, they are consigned to the past and cannot be repeated. If, on the other hand, these are idealized episodes illustrating universal demands, every hearer of the gospel must give ear.

We have shown that the pericope of the rich man, by its structure and its immediate context, is a "paradigm," an example (whether based on fact or not) of a conduct proposed for all (see p. 67). The passage on the absolute character of the disciple's vocation enunciates no concrete demand; one must be ready to follow the master by renouncing "all" security, and to do so immediately at the expense of even the most sacred family duties (see pp. 30–31). It is possible that such sayings could have been pronounced strictly for the disciples, but they really only affirm the absolute primacy of the person of Jesus and the urgency of his call. Thus they have a more universal character and value.

Luke's repetition of the command "Go, sell what you have" is placed each time in an explicitly universal context (see pp. 66–67). Thus these texts, which at first seem particular, ultimately must be placed in the general category, for their message challenges all the readers of the Gospels.

4. TO GIVE UP ONE'S POSSESSIONS—A CALL FOR EVERYONE?

This summary reminder allows us to answer the question: Do the Synoptics address the demand to give up one's possessions (to share them with others) to all believers? We unhesitatingly must say Yes. There is no ambiguity in the texts. It would be good, nonetheless, first to indicate the different opinions of exegetes on the subject.

A good many exegetes are of the opinion that the invitation to renounce one's possessions and family could have been directed at only the limited group of disciples, and henceforth has merely historical value, since this type of "disciple" no longer exists.[2] This perspective would eliminate all problems, since the demand is seen as no longer relevant.

We note once again that what is at stake in this discussion, is, first, the surrendering of one's possessions and, second, of one's family. But, as we have observed, such demands are never direct historical calls. When they are explicit (the case of the rich man and Luke's texts), their contexts generalize them.

However, to base everything on pure historicity is neither obvious nor completely satisfying, since many indications suggest that the texts are more widely relevant. Other exegetes attempt to reserve the demands for a particular group of people. This group would be not only the historical disciples but also a special core group of the primitive community: men and women entrusted with a function of ministerial service (*amtsträger*), predecessors of the ministerial body of the church, "successors" of the apostles such as the evangelists, prophets, and itinerant missionaries.[3] They extend the ministry of the twelve and continue their lifestyle, particularly by renouncing possessions and family. One cannot deny that this exegetical position has a certain logic about it. If the radical instructions were addressed only to the twelve (or to the special disciples in the larger sense of the word) and if nonetheless they must have permanent validity, they are best applied to those ensuring the continuity of the apostolic function. Thus it is not the logic of this hypothesis that is weak; it simply lacks an objective textual basis. No texts authorize us to envisage a special elite for whom certain demands would be reserved.

Other exegetes see in Jesus' community (the twelve) and in his demands expressed in the texts on renunciation, material possessions, and so forth (demands addressed also to themselves), a kind of prefiguration of the phenomenon of religious life (which appeared in an organized communal form only after the fourth century A.D.). These religious communities would take upon themselves the radical instructions of the Gospels.[4] This view comes close to distinguishing between precepts and counsels—for example, the invitation to perfection in the text "if you wish to be perfect" (Matt. 19:21) would be interpreted as desirable but optional.

Such a position leaves the field of exegesis and enters into historical interpretation. Let us say clearly that this opinion seems to be without any exegetical foundation. For if there is a "succession" to the twelve (and the other original disciples), the claim cannot be made by the religious, but must be made by ministers and elders. Yet the decisive argument against such a point of view is the fact that nothing in the texts examined allows for the radical demands to be reserved to any limited group whatsoever.

We conclude that the Synoptics extend these demands, including the sharing of goods, to all believers, to all those who, after

Easter will be called disciples. These demands are often clear-cut and blunt. How to live them out concretely, though, remains a disturbing, ongoing challenge to creativity.

NOTES

1. This is the moderate and sensible conclusion of Hengel, *Nachfolge und Charisma* (Berlin: Töpelmann, 1968), pp. 94–99.

2. Thus Braun, *Spätjüdisch—häretischer und Früchristlicher Radikalismus,* 2 vols. (Tübingen: J. C. B. Mohr, 1969), 2:74–76; Schulz, *Nachfogen und Nachame* (Munich: Kösel-Verlag, 1962), pp. 94–97.

3. Degenhardt, *Lukas* (Stuttgart: Kath. Bibelwerk, 1965), pp. 215–21.

4. This is the position of H. Schürmann, "Le groupe des disciples de Jésus," *Christus* 50 (1966): 184–209, which the full title of the article indicates: "The group of Jesus' disciples, a sign for Israel and prototype of the life according to the counsels."

12

The Relevance of Radicalism

Until now our study and our reflections were limited to the field of exegesis, though occasionally the applications for today were noted. As we near the conclusion of our study, let us raise current problems that Christians living today in this moment of history are confronting. Whoever believes in the unique message of Jesus and believes that the essence of this message is contained in a privileged way in the writings of the New Testament, particularly in the Gospels, would also consider it to be of supreme importance to discern how this message continues, with more or less intimacy, to address itself to the believer today.

Certainly one cannot remain indifferent to the question of radicalism, since the term is constantly used in a multitude of contexts. The readers will perhaps be disappointed that we have not discussed the political aspect of Jesus' message, since in the Anglo-Saxon milieu "radical" and "radicalism," even in a religious context, frequently have such a connotation. For us this is a completely different subject, which, because of the angle of our approach, chosen and justified at the beginning, remains outside the field of our investigation.

RADICALISM: REVEALING THE ABSOLUTE CHARACTER OF THE MESSAGE

The radical demands situated in the totality of Jesus' message are not simply added elements or options meant for an elite;

rather, they reveal the unchanging core of this sharp, cutting message. They do not exist in isolation, but force whoever encounters them to the shocking, unfathomable, all-consuming words of Jesus. To affirm that, one must place Jesus at the center of everything. That one must love one's neighbor with the tender mercy of God, that this love rejects all inequality and rejoices in sharing is a noble affirmation to which everyone would assent, but few actually weigh the extreme practical consequences of such an affirmation.

The radical demands of Jesus strip bare, in full view, the fundamental meaning of these choices. The primacy of Jesus and his call requires that we prefer him to our possessions, family, physical life, and our very personhood. The love of neighbor must go beyond kindness, generosity, mutual support, and forgiveness to the love of one's enemies. It will not tolerate some being deprived while others have an abundance of the world's goods.

With radicalism thus situated in the whole message of Jesus, as a point of intersection with real life and with the issue of possessions and sharing in proper perspective, then the question of knowing to whom these radical demands are addressed seems to resolve itself. Jesus challenges the believer to feel the almost crushing weight of the core of the gospel: to believe, to hand oneself over to Jesus, to accept the new existence entails much more than modifying theoretical viewpoints. This choice overturns and shatters the individual's concrete existence, relational network, lifestyle, attachments, everything. And this is but a logical consequence of the initial choice, the Yes to the unpredictable adventure of faith.

UTOPIA OR REALITY?

This entire scope of Jesus' radical demands can be summed up, as we have said, in a few essential points: the primacy of Jesus, unconditional love of neighbor, freedom vis-à-vis possessions, and sharing with the poor. The fact remains that these are exorbitant, frightening demands before which one feels small and poor, if not powerless.

However, even when placed in their context and setting, even when "explained," they are still disturbing. There is always the temptation to diffuse their glare and leave them vacuous. One can exegete them to death and kill all their intensity so that the only thing left is conventional wisdom. Or else—and this has often happened in the history of Christendom—a chosen group is set aside to practice radicalism, relieving the masses of believers from any such responsibility.

In practice people have oscillated between utopian and literal interpretations. Literalism—that is, harsh and immediate application of all the instructions—has caused some men to castrate themselves in order to become "eunuchs for the sake of the kingdom," to make celibacy a prerequisite to Christian baptism, to impose a regimented, total communism upon all the baptized.[1]

Utopia, if taken positively, consists in acknowledging that the proposals should be accomplished while admitting that one can only go to a certain point. The practice is not a literal one, but neither is it simply a pious, ineffective wish. When the situation warrants it, one will have to risk one's life for Christ and, above all, to accept his demands daily, even if one meets opposition from one's family or one's own self. The equality of all, sharing of material possessions, mutual support, and forgiveness will be unceasingly sought for and lived out in fraternal communion. Of course, one will constantly be confronted with one's limits and those of others; one will not be able to live up to the ideal constantly; one will constantly fail. But also, one will not declare that the undertaking is impossible or that one should give it up to another, more dedicated person. Instead, he or she will live with the tension and the reproach associated with this ever present yet never completely attainable ideal. Radicalism taken seriously creates a tension without which Christian life stagnates. It is the disturbing element necessary for the dynamism; it is the dissatisfaction that becomes expectation of what is to come but is not yet.

Rather than alleviate the pain through soothing exegesis, rather than relegating it to a favored "elect" with a special calling, the Christian accepts being disturbed, dissatisfied, troubled, and never completely at home with this inexhaustible demand because it is impossible to regiment or measure it. This radicalism challenges all Christians and ignites their zeal to dream the impossible and search for their heart's desire, which will never be found until the definitive arrival of the kingdom. It is a utopia that does not drain one's energies but gives fuller life.

FOR MANY OR FOR FEW?

It was a great misfortune when, after attempts to apply radicalism literally for an entire community failed, many began imperceptibly to think that only some Christians were called to live it.[2] Taking the entire gospel as the highest norm of one's life, striving day by day to respond to it despite the inadequacies of one's response, unceasingly hoping in the mercy of God, living together as a community in prayer, sharing materially—all ended by becoming a special vocation of those more "perfect," and thus not a vocation for the common person. Sharing possessions, which assumes a community, became a counsel; a radicalism wrongly emphasizing one aspect of the use of possessions remains to this day associated only with those who commit themselves to religious life, as shown in the literature consecrated to it. Do not recent writings define the religious life as more or less having a monopoly on gospel radicalism? We hope that this present study will have shown how partial and incorrect such a position is. Gospel radicality taken as a whole, situated in its proper setting, and correctly understood is not—either in the New Testament or today—the prerogative of any particular group. It involves all believers equally. If Christians had been more attentive to this fact in the past, if we were more attentive to it today, the face of Christianity would be different, nearer to what Jesus wanted. May this present study contribute to our renewed vigilance.

NOTES

1. In the first centuries of Christianity (2nd–4th), there were some claims of a literal practice of the logion on eunuchs—claims that, moreover, disapprove of it. The case of Origen remains a debated one. For the claims, see H. Baltensweiler, *Die Ehe im Neuen Testament* (Zurich: Zwingli, 1967), pp. 106–7.

The vow of celibacy as a preliminary condition for baptism was practiced in the second century in certain rigorous Syrian communities: G. Kretschmar, "Ein Betrag zur Frage nach dem Ursprung Frühchristlicher Askese," *Zeitschrift für Theologie und Kirche* 61 (1964): 29, 64. Total communal sharing of goods was the dream (and the practice) of Thomas Münzer, John de Leyde, and their partisans in the sixteenth century.

2. On this failure, especially in Syrian communities, and on its consequences, see Kretschmar, "Ein Betrag," pp. 64–67.

Bibliography

Indicated here are books and articles used in this study of evangelical radicalism. First of all, as basic, is

Aland, K. *Synopsis quattuor evangeliorum*. 8th ed. Stuttgart: Würtembergische Bibelanstalt, 1973.

1. Comparative Exegetical Analysis of the Synoptic Gospels

Benoît, B. and Boismard, M. E. *Synopse de quatre évangiles en français*. Vol. 2, *Commentaire*. Paris: Cerf, 1972.

Bultmann, Rudolf. *Die Geschichte der synoptischen Tradition*. 7th ed. Göttingen: Vandenhoek and Ruprecht, 1967. English translation, *History of the Synoptic Tradition*. New York: Harper & Row, 1963.

Manson, T.W. *The Sayings of Jesus as Recorded in the Gospels According to St. Matthew and St. Luke*. New edition. Naperville, Ill.: Allenson, 1949, and London: SCM Press, 1971.

2. Studies Directly Related to Radicalism

Braun, Herbert. *Spätjüdische—häretischer und früchristlicher Radikalismus*. 2nd ed. Two volumes. Tübingen: Mohr, 1969.

Minear, Paul. *Commands of Christ: Authority and Implications*. Nashville: Abingdon, 1972.

Rigaux, Beda. "Le radicalisme du Règne." In *La pauvreté évangélique*. Lire la Bible, 27, pp. 135–73. Paris: Cerf, 1971. English translation, "The Radicalism of the Kingdom." In *Gospel Poverty*, pp. 916–55. Chicago: Franciscan Herald Press, 1977.

3. Other Studies Relating to the Theme

Aerts, Th. "Suivre Jesus." *Ephemerides Theologicae Lovanienses* 42 (1966): 476–512.

Betz, H.D. *Nachfolge und Nachahmung Jesu Christi im Neuen Testament.* Tübingen: Mohr, 1967.

Davies, William D. *The Setting of the Sermon on the Mount.* Cambridge University Press, 1964.

Degenhardt, H. J. *Lukas—Evangelist der Armen.* Stuttgart: Kath. Bibelwerk, 1965.

Denis, A. M. "Ascèse et vie chrétienne." *Revue des Sciences Théologiques et Philosophiques* 47 (1963): 606–18.

Dinkler, E. "Jesus Wort vom Kreuztragen." In *Neutestamentliche Studien für Rudolf Bultmann*, pp. 110–29. Berlin (BZNW 21) 1954.

Dupont, Jacques. "Renoncer à tous ses beins." *Nouvelle Revue Théologique* 93 (1971): 563–82.

———. "Les pauvres et le pauvreté dans les évangiles et les Actes." In *La pauvreté évangélique*, Lire la Bible, 27, pp. 37–52. Paris: Cerf, 1971.

———. *Les Béatitudes.* Études Biblique, 3 vols. Paris: Gabalda, 1973.

Hengel, Martin. *Nachfolge und Charisma.* Berlin: Töpelmann, 1968.

Kretschmar, G. "Ein Beitrag zur Frage nach dem Ursprung früchristlicher Askese." *Zeitschrift für Theologie und Kirche* 61 (1964): 27–67.

Légasse, S. *L'appel du riche.* Paris: Beauchesne, 1966. Resumé article "L'appel du riche," in *La pauvreté évangélique*, Lire la Bible, 27, pp. 65–91. Paris: Cerf, 1971.

———. *Jésus et l'enfant.* Etudes Bibliques. Paris: Cerf, 1969.

Neuhäusler, E. *Exigence de Dieu et Morale chrétienne.* Translated from German. Paris: Cerf, 1971.

Percy, Ernst. *Die Botschaft Jesu.* Lund: Gleerup, 1953.

Schnackenburg, Rudolf. *Die Sittliche Botschaft des Neuen Testament.* Munich: M. Hüber, 1954. English translation, *The Moral Teaching of the New Testament.* Translated by J. Holland-Smith and W. J. O'Hara. New York: Herder and Herder, 1965, and Crossroad, 1973.

Schulz, A. *Nachfolgen und Nachamen*. Munich: Kosel, 1962.

Schürmann, H. "Le groupe des disciples du Jésus." *Christus* 50 (1966): 184–209.

Van Canghe, J. M. "Fondement évangélique de la vie religieuse." *Nouvelle Revue Theologique* 95 (1973): 635–47.

Von Campenhausen, Hans. *Die Askese in Urchristentum*. Tübingen: Mohr, 1967.

Index of Scriptural References